MW00416128

Current of My Life Fishing

A BICULTURAL, BILINGUAL RESEARCH SCIENTIST WHO LED A CURIOSITY-DRIVEN, SATISFYING LIFE UNDER SHADOW OF THE JAPAN-USA RELATIONSHIP

Robert Kanji Fujimura

ISBN: 1-4811-7475-4
ISBN-13: 978-1-4811-7475-6
Library of Congress Control Number: 2013906828
CreateSpace Independent Publishing Platform
North Charleston, South Carolina

For my children, Dan, Tomi, and Kei; my siblings, June, Irene, and Jerry; and those interested in the history of the relationship between Japan and the United States

TABLE OF CONTENT

ACKNOWLEDGEMENT

This autobiography was written primarily for my wife, children, and siblings.

I thank my wife for continuous support throughout our marriage and teaching me about Japanese etiquette.

I thank my children, Dan, Tomi, and Kei, and my siblings, Jerry, Irene, and June, for providing me with information whenever I sought it.

I thank Prof. Tetsuden Kashima, Department of American Ethnic Studies, University of Washington, Seattle WA. He had induced me to write the memoirs for wider readership. I thank Gary A. Wedemeyer PhD (Ret.), Senior Scientist Emeritus, US Geological Survey Western Fisheries Research Center, Seattle; Adjunct Professor (Ret.), University of Washington. He is a friend at University Temple United Methodist Church, who had carefully read and edited the last version prior to the final draft of this manuscript and encouraged me to publish it.

PROLOGUE

This is the memoir of my life from the day of the attack on Pearl Harbor, the event that determined the course of my life, to the election and reelection of a man of color, Barack Obama, as president of the United States of America. This memoir is interwoven with the history of the Japan-US relationship, which affected me throughout my life. During my lifetime. I lived in Japan, or her proper, from the Japan-China War to the Great Far East War to the complete defeat of the Japanese militaristic regime. I observed her recovery from the ruin to become the second largest economy in the world and the rise of China under Communism to replace Japan as the number two economy. Then I observed in person the struggle of the Japanese to recover from the life-changing event of the current generation—the Great Earthquake of East Japan on March 11, 2011.

When I became aware of the world around me in Manchuria, located in the northeast corner of China, the United States and Japan were at war, hating each other and trying to kill each other. Subsequently, I lived under the friendly alliance of the United States and Japan, each claiming the other, at one time or another, as its most important ally.

During the early period of modernization, Japan fought wars to prevent being colonized, but for more than sixty years after the Pacific War, Japan lived under the protective umbrella of the United States. Now, near the end of my life, Japan could no longer depend on America to maintain peace with neighbors of Japan. She should get out from the umbrella and actively strive for peace and harmony, and seek cooperation among Pacific nations.

Sukeichi Fujimura, my grandfather, came to the United States from a farm near Yamaguchi City (the capital of Yamaguchi Prefecture at the southwest end of Honshu). He first went to Hawaii with his next-door neighbor Tsuda in the 1890s. They probably went as contract workers in sugar cane fields. Sukeichi was the second son of the family and probably did not have much of a future as a farmer. Traditionally, the eldest son of the family inherited the farm, and the rest of the sons had to do something else. Farmers were poor and had difficulty making their living.

On May 5, 1904 (about three months after the beginning of Russo-Japanese War), they came to the United States, entering the Port of Tacoma, Washington. They watched as Mount Rainier came closer and closer; Japanese immigrants of that period called that mountain Tacoma Fuji. It was as majestic as Mount Fuji. My grandfather and Tsuda probably used Hawaii as a stepping-stone to come to America, as many early Japanese immigrants did.

He opened a barbershop. According to the available records, he never worked for anyone after coming to America. Apparently, he was doing well by 1912 and went back to Yamaguchi to get married. Most of the Japanese could not afford to travel back to Japan to get married; they got married by exchanging photos. Chiyo Tanaka was induced to marry Sukeichi by her stepmother, who was Sukeichi's aunt. Her name was entered into the Fujimura Family Registry as married on April 3, 1912, the official way for the Japanese to get married. Chiyo was trained as a nurse and was nineteen years old, twelve years younger than her husband. Chiyo's family was wealthy; they were tile makers in Hofu. Taiichiro Tanaka, her father, is etched in one of the stone plaques at Hofu Tenmangu, the city's Shinto shrine. Chiyo used to brag to us, her grandchildren that her family owned a large rice field that she walked on it all the way to school. In feudal Japan the family wealth was measured by the amount of rice produced on the family property. She implied that she made a large sacrifice by marrying a farmer's son. Actually, farmers had higher social status than businessmen in Feudal Japan. The society looked down on people who worked to make money.

My grandparents had only one child, a daughter, Tamiko Ruth, who was born on March 14, 1914. They were too busy with their business; therefore, they sent Tamiko to Chiyo's parents in Hofu. According to the port of entry record, Tamiko was in Japan from 1917 to 1920.

Chiyo went back to Japan to get Tamiko prior to her entry into grade school. Then Chiyo refused to come back unless her husband changed the business from a barbershop to a hotel. Sukeichi acquired Detroit Hotel situated at Ninth Avenue and Howell Street near Olive Way. The hotel was probably on lease because the Japanese without citizenships could not buy a property, and the Japanese were not qualified to obtain citizenship. They were well-to-do, and Tamiko got everything she wanted except love and affection, which she frequently complained about to her children later in her life.

Grandmother was a strong-willed woman and became the matriarch of the Fujimura family. Tamiko Ruth was the only child, and Grandmother decided to follow a Japanese custom and she adopted a son by her daughter's marriage. Grandmother chose her cousin, Tatsuo Kawamura, as their adopted son without informing Tamiko of her intension. He came from Hofu; they knew each other prior to Chiyo's emigration from Japan. By the time Tatsuo came to the United States (1931), the Japanese were no longer able to get a permanent visa because of the discriminatory immigration law against them. Therefore, he came as a student at the University of Washington. He already had a law degree from Kansai University in Osaka but entered the University of Washington as a political science major (1932). His transcript shows poor grades, suggesting his primary purpose was to get married.

During his stay in Seattle, he taught in a Japanese school. The Japanese American community had a weekend school where many Nisei learned to speak, read, and write Japanese; Tamiko was one of them. Tamiko was told by her mother to get married to Tatsuo soon after she graduated from high school. This was the first time Tamiko heard that she had to marry him. They got married on June 14, 1931. She was seventeen.

Tatsuo graduated in 1936 and had to leave the country. By that time, he had two children, — Kanji Robert, born on July 28, 1933, and Minako June, born on June 29, 1935. The family is shown at the Detroit Hotel in the photo on the right, taken just prior to leaving for Japan. I am the little boy in the sailor shirt. Tatsuo's family accompanied him to Japan.

Fujimura family at Detroit Hotel

The family stayed with Tatsuo's parents in Hofu, but soon his wife conceived another child. Tamiko went back to Seattle to give birth to the child (1937); Minako and Kanji went with her. Their second daughter, Yoko Irene, was born on January 10, 1938.

By the time Tamiko and her children came back to Seattle, her parents had moved to a bigger hotel, Diller

Hotel, on First Avenue and University Street, within walking distance from Pike Market. According to Grandmother they had thriving business, often overflowing with sailors who slept along the hallways. In 1942 they were forced to vacate the hotel and move to Camp Minidoka, one of the concentration camps for people of Japanese ethnicity. *Now the building is an apartment for artists, and the space adjacent to the entrance is the Diller Room, an old-style bar. The building is designated as a historical site, built in 1890; Seattle Art Museum is located across the street.*

Father apparently had problems finding a job in Japan because of the depression and went to Dairen (Dalian), a port at the southern tip of Kwantung Province (Liaodong Peninsula) off Manchuko, and sought assistance of Hasegawa Teizo, brother-in-law of his eldest brother, to find a job (1938). Hasegawa Teizo, an Osaka merchant, had a construction company in Dalian; he was wealthy and had a beautiful home on the slope of a hill. Many young Japanese men of that period went to Manchuko to seek jobs and adventures.

The Japanese had Kwantung Province on a ninety-nine-year lease from Qing dynasty after the Russo-Japanese War (1904–1905); Russians had the province on a similar lease prior to the war. After that war the Japanese also gained control of the Manchuria Railway, built by the Russians, and established Mantetsu, a semiprivate company, to operate the railroad. The Kwantung Army, a Japanese army, guarded Mantetsu from Chinese and Manchu warlords. The Japanese expanded the railway network and built a high-speed train named Ajia (Asia). *The Shinkansen, bullet trains built in Japan after World War II, were modeled after Ajia with further improvements on the design of the rails and locomotives; now the trains are controlled by computers.*

In 1931 the staff of the Kwantung Army led by Itagaki Taisuke and Ishihara Kanji ordered a unit of the army to explode the railroad near Shenyang (Manchu incident). The incident was blamed on a Chinese warlord. The Kwantung Army used it as an excuse to occupy the whole Manchuria and established Manchuko. The last emperor of the Qing Dynasty, Pu Yi, was enthroned as the emperor of Manchuko in 1934. By using a similar tactic, the Japanese Army in North China started the war from a small incident near Beijing on July 7, 1937. The Japanese side considered this as the beginning of the war against China.

Father found a job with the hotel division of Mantetsu, which had a chain of hotels named Yamato Hotel located in major cities along the railroad where VIPs stayed. In 1939 Father moved to the administrative department of Yamato Hotel in Hoten or Mukden (the present name is Shenyang, which at that time was the name of one of the boroughs of Hoten) and asked his family to join him. Therefore, we moved to Manchuko when China and Japan were already at war. My father made his family move to such a place from peaceful Seattle. *I do not understand what he was thinking. He was a graduate of political science from the University of Washington, and I am sure he was aware that Japan was fighting a war against China. The relationship between the United States and Japan was getting worse and worse.*

The Fujimura family settled in Yamato, one of the boroughs of Hoten resided in by Japanese. Manchuko was peaceful, but a full scale war was going on in the mainland of China.

This memoir starts from my life in Hoten.

Notes on the conventions I followed: Names of the Japanese were written with the last name followed by the first name except for our relatives whom I called by their first names. The dates on the Pacific side are the Japan time. Names of the Chinese places are Japanese names used at the time I lived there. I introduced the spelling used in the World Map of National Geographic, 2010, whenever available; others were in Chinese phonetics.

PART I:

A STUDENT IN JAPANESE SCHOOLS IN MANCHURIA AND JAPAN

CHAPTER 1:
THE PEARL HARBOR ATTACK

On the morning of December 8, 1941 (all the dates are in Japan time on the other side of the Pacific), I was awoken by the news that the Japanese Imperial Navy had attacked Pearl Harbor, destroying four battleships and sinking and damaging many others while losing only twenty-nine planes and five suicidal midget submarines.

I was in the second grade at Aoi Kokumin Gakko (a Japanese primary School) in Hoten (Shenyang), Manchuko (Northeast China). In the school auditorium that morning, the message from the emperor was read to us that the Japanese had declared war on the United States. and Britain and that the war could not have been averted. From that day on, until the end of the war, we heard the emperor's message on the eighth of every month. Whether the war could not have been averted was the question I had in my mind throughout my life, and I integrated my perception on impacts of America on modern Japan in postscript to this autobiography, which is my version of history of the Japan-US relationship.

Initial victories by the Japanese were astounding to the people of both sides. The Japanese battle plans were bold and executed perfectly. The Japanese military forces simultaneously attacked Pearl Harbor, the Philippines, Malay, Indonesia, and Burma. They occupied the Philippines, Malay Peninsula, Singapore, Indonesia and Burma swiftly; therefore, they had accomplished their objective within the first year. The Japanese people were jubilant and believed they could defeat any enemy with Yamato Damashii, Japanese spirit, even with insufficient weapons.

In reality only the Americans in the Philippines led by General MacArthur fought back but were defeated. The resistance by the British, Dutch, and French forces was almost nonexistent. The British had an "unsinkable" battleship, Prince of Wales, and its companion, Repulse; they were sunk at the first encounter. The Japanese force led by General Yamashita occupied "infallible" Singapore by invading swiftly from Malay, the side that was not fortified. General MacArthur left the Philippines saying, "I shall return."

The Americans heard the news in disbelief: how little, yellow Japs with weapons made from materials mostly imported from America could inflict so much damage simultaneously at so many fronts! "Remember Pearl Harbor" became their battle cry. The Japanese misjudged the American character and the outcome of the war in

4

Europe. They thought the Germans would win the war, and the Americans would lose the will to fight alone in the Pacific. The American leaders were aware that the war was imminent but thought by stopping sales of oil and scrap irons, the Japanese would back down. Instead, the Japanese started the war, even though they did not have much confidence that they could win.

I was ostracized at my school as an American. Until the Pearl Harbor attack, I was not conscious of my nationality.

I did not know, until after getting back to America after the war, that all the Japanese Americans from the Pacific Coast were sent to internment camps in the spring of 1942. My grandparents, Sukeichi and Chiyo went to the camp at Minidoka, Idaho, and lost their hotel, Diller Hotel, at First Avenue and University Street. "Minidoka Interlude" (Takeuchi, 1989) shows the photo of the group with our grandparents adjacent to the Block Thirty-Eight, barrack twelve. My Grandparents stayed there until they learned they could get out as long as they did not go back to the West Coast. I think they got out prior to the end of the war, but I could not find the record. That internment period was the only time in my grandfather's life that he was able to relax and pursue his hobby. He liked woodworks, and he brought out of the camp a lamp stand made of driftwood, which I remembered seeing in his house after the war.

CHAPTER 2:
SHENYANG

Prior to the day of infamy (a famous saying of President Franklin Roosevelt), I do not remember much, except that the neighborhood kids would visit, and my siblings and I would share our candies and our toys sent by our grandparents in America. We had more toys and candies than the rest of the kids in the neighborhood combined. Our neighbors played with our toys more than we did; I preferred to read books. I did enjoy playing with my Lionel electric train set; it had passenger cars, a station, and a tunnel. We felt America was a very rich nation full of candies and toys. I made a sled from redwood boards off a crate; it was the best sled I ever had.

We went to visit Hasegawa in Dalian at the tip of Liaodong Peninsula twice. Hasegawa had a beautiful two-story, white house with a glass-enclosed patio on the slope of a hill. Hasegawa had a son, Sadakazu, and two daughters, Kimi and Sadayo—all older than I. *I will be indebted to them later in my life.* Sadakazu liked to build model airplanes and boats. We went to Hoshigaura, a famous beach nearby and played with his boat. He also liked to collect insects. He showed me boxes of them and taught me their names. They had at least three white, medium-sized dogs. They also had about three maids taking care of chores around the house.

My brother, Shogo Jerry, was born in Shenyang only about six months before the war, June 2, 1941. We got a maid from Hasegawas to help our mother. She was the youngest maid of Hasegawas and often asked me to scrub her back when she bathed. In a Japanese style bath, furo, one washed oneself outside of the tub. I probably remember it because she was a young but chubby woman. I do not know how long she stayed, but she was gone by time of the Pearl Harbor attack.

Just before the war (September 1941), my father was promoted to manager of the Yamato Hotel in Hailar near the Siberian border. At first Father was in Hailar by himself, leaving the rest of his family in Shenyang. Thus, when the war started, we were in Shenyang separated from our father. I think our mother felt isolated in the hostile neighborhood. She was the only one in the neighborhood with Western style dress and makeup; other women in the neighborhood wore kimonos tucked into overalls made of old cotton kimonos and wore no makeup. Our father must not have thought about the possibility of the Japan-America war and must have trusted the nonaggression treaty between Japan and Russia when he accepted the position as the manager of Hailar Yamato

Hotel, leaving his family behind. Apparently, he could not find a suitable place for his family to live. He may have known that for his wife, Hailar was too desolate with no entertainment or a shopping district.

In retrospect his move was very puzzling because he majored in political science at the University of Washington and should have been aware of a possible Japan-America war. Francis G. Wilson, a professor of political science during the time my father was a student, wrote in his book that "in the Far East we did not wish to see Japan become a stronger power by the conquest of China" (1949). The Japanese were moving deeper and deeper into China. I do not remember my father ever telling me his view on the war; perhaps I was too young.

Shenyang was the largest city in Manchuko (population 1.3 million around that time). We lived in Yamato-ku (Hagimachi 48-6-2), the Japanese section of the city, in an apartment in a multiple-unit, two-story building, the overview shaped like a square bracket. We were in one of the first floor units with individual entrances to the street. The second floor units had an entrance to the veranda in the back that led to the stairway. The unit had tatami floors (rice straw mat; the most preferred floor for the Japanese) and modern facilities with a gas range and flush toilet. Mantetsu probably managed the apartments.

The unit was heated by a pechka, (a Russian style cylindrical column coal furnace) situated in the center of the unit with a sector exposed to each room. The rooms were full of flies; walls were brownish from their feces. Sticky strips hanging from lampshades were covered with flies within a few days. The area was peaceful and safe, but thieves broke into our house twice. After the second time, a Manchurian came to our house and asked if we had any more jewels. I think our mother said no, and that stopped the break-ins.

There was a Japanese shopping district with a large department store. We went there frequently, usually on a horse-drawn carriage. It was common to argue with the drivers over price after the passengers got off (I think the drivers just liked to argue. If we quietly paid the asking price, they did not look happy). There were taxis, but they were not a common means of travel, and there were no public mass transit systems. After the war started, a charcoal furnace attached to the back of the car replaced the gasoline engine. I assume the steam from the furnace powered the car. I remember also walking frequently to a nearby bakery to buy bread. We ate bread more than the average Japanese did. Rice was rationed, and our neighbors were complaining that they did not have enough rice, but we had more than we could consume. The rice would get old and had worms in it sometimes, and I remember mother getting rid of them while washing the rice prior to cooking it.

We went to see movies once in a while. The only live show I remember seeing was a magician in an auditorium. The performer claimed he had two stomachs and could regurgitate an object from one of them. I remember he swallowed a whole egg, cracked the shell, and removed the shells from his mouth. He performed with his upper body naked to show there were no hidden tricks.

He said customs officials knew about him, and he was x-rayed every time at the port of entry. We did not go out to eat very often, but I do remember going to a restaurant inside a gas company office building and having suki-yaki cooked at an individual table.

Our father came back from Hailar occasionally and brought back balls of Russian cheese about half the size of a bowling ball and boxes of chocolates with liquor in them. The cheeses were sharp, and we did not eat much. Father probably had them with his drinks. I assume he brought vodka with him, because he liked strong drinks.

We were in Shenyang until I was in the fourth grade. I had the best childhood period in Shenyang. We played with neighborhood kids in our inner court of the apartments until dark whenever we could. I do not remember the specifics, but we played kick the can, hide-and-seek, and several nameless games without any adult supervision. We played baseball with any ball and stick we could find. We used thin metal sheets as the bases, and I once cut my right foot while sliding into a base. I still have a visible scar from the injury. I remember the names of only a couple of my friends—Manabu, who acted like my older brother, and Miyako, a tomboy who would occasionally chase after me and wrestle me down. The open side of the inner court had a high wooden fence, which we could climb up to get out. Initially, the other side of the fence was a wide-open, grass covered field. We could see beautiful sunsets accompanied often by a huge number of crows flying by, making noise. Apparently, it was a common sight; there was a Japanese

11

children's song about crows flying at sunset—"crow, crow why you cry?"

I remember, probably soon after the beginning of the war, new houses being built on the field. Bricks were made on site. The house adjacent to the fence was a Western style, single-unit house owned by the Todas. The family had a son a year or two younger than I was. I went to his house often, and we listened to sumo tournaments together. Sumo was the only sport I listened to, and Futabayama usually won the tournaments. *He is a legend in sumo; he won sixty-nine sumo matches straight from the spring of 1936 to the spring of 1938, which is still a record. During that period, there were only two tournaments per year lasting eleven or thirteen days per tournament; now there are six lasting fifteen days each.* The only specific happening during the sumo tournaments that I remember was the time Admiral Yamamoto Isoroku was killed when his airplane was shot down over Bougainville Island in the Solomons. His death was announced during the spring sumo tournament in 1943. He was famous for planning and executing the attack at Pearl Harbor. I rushed outside to tell the other kids, but they did not believe me.

The Americans had cracked the Japanese military code and waited for the plane carrying Yamamoto to fly over the island and shot his plane down. Yamamoto may have wished to die and exposed himself to unnecessary dangers. He predicted that he could control the sea and air for about a year, implying that Japan should quit the war by then. By the time he was killed, Japan had lost the control of the sea and air by a series of battles near the Solomon Islands. All the subsequent battles were defensive battles as the American forces attacked from island to island of their choice toward Tokyo. I think Yamamoto felt he did the best he could and was willing to die to get out of the hopeless situation. Traditionally, the Japanese leaders committed suicide when they were defeated.

CHAPTER 3:
HAILAR

During the summer of 1943, we moved to Hailar to join our father. It is a major city near the northwest border to Siberia with a population of about forty thousand; after the war it became a part of Inner Mongolia. Hailar was on a basin by the eastern edge of the Gobi desert. There were camels on the streets with Mongolian nomads in native costumes; I think they were the majority in that area. A few Japanese soldiers in uniform were often walking around; Hailar was the only place we saw Japanese soldiers. Russian women were throwing away buckets full of water in the ditch by a road. I do not remember seeing many Chinese.

The winter was very cold, at least minus forty degrees. (At that temperature it is the same in both Celsius and Fahrenheit; so it's a convenient temperature to remember.) Hailar was the only place where I had to wear a fur hat, a fur coat, and a pair of wool boots. The first day it got cold, I was wearing only an American made wool jacket and a pair of earmuffs. My teacher was shocked and took me home on a horse-drawn carriage. During the weather change in the spring, it was often windy and sand blew from the surrounding sand dunes, and we had to wear eye goggles outside.

We lived in a Russian style house; the outside walls were finished with large rocks cemented to the walls. Two bedrooms were converted to tatami floors where we slept on futons. The house had a furnished living room and dining room. It also had a large family room and a study, but we used them for storage. The house was heated by at least three pechkas. These were not efficient heaters, so we were cold, and we often leaned against the walls during the winter for warmth. I made the entire backyard into a vegetable garden. I guess it was about thirty feet by twenty feet, the largest one we had in Manchuria. The house had a patio enclosed by windows, where we stored coal purchased four tons at a time. The kitchen had a large coal stove and a well with a reservoir above the sink. It became Father's exercise machine to pump water into the water reservoir. The pump had a handle shaped like a baseball bat, which he pushed forward and back. I helped sometimes. Mother may have pumped it in the beginning, but she got caries, tuberculosis of a bone, in her fourth finger on her left hand. It was puffed up and braced. She did not pump it after that. Beneath the kitchen was a cellar where we kept potatoes, cabbages, and onions over the winter. This was the only house we lived while in Manchuria; the rest were apartments. That was the only house I remember that had a telephone.

I do not remember going to a commercial district. Our mother went to a place, which looked like a storage place, and ordered items she wanted at the counter. She complained that there was no entertainment, not even a place to do window-shopping.

I do not understand why Father made us move to Hailar when the Japanese were obviously losing the war. Apparently, he trusted that the Russians would honor the treaty and would not invade Manchuko. Maybe he thought the Russians were too worn out to open a new front in Asia even against the weakened Kwantung Army. I heard that many soldiers from the Kwantung Army were transferred to the South Pacific or to the Japanese homeland.

Our neighbors in Hailar lived in single-unit houses that were more spread out than the place we lived in Shenyang. I remember only a girl living across the street from us, but we never played. I went fishing a couple of times with my classmate Yoshida Tetsuo. One day we did not catch anything, and as we walked back, Yoshida told me that something terrible must have happened and that was the reason we did not catch anything. A few minutes after we got back, he told me over the phone that his father was killed in an accident. His father was an electrician, and he was up on one of the poles to take off the electric wires because the pole was rotten and needed to be replaced. While he was still up near the top of the pole, it fell to the ground killing him.

His family took his ashes back to Saga, Japan. I remember the name of the prefecture because the champion of one of the sumo tournaments around that year was Saganohana, which means a flower from Saga Prefecture in Kyushu. I never heard from Yoshida again; his family may have been killed on the ferry that sunk between Korea and Kyushu; American submarines sank many ferries around that period.

CHAPTER 4:
QIQIHAR

We stayed in Hailar about a year and then moved to Qiqihar (1944), a city of 170,000 located southeast of Hailar on the other side of the major mountain range of Koanrei (Greater Khingan Range). We stayed in the Japanese residential district in Qiqihar in a duplex apartment. It had four tatami rooms, a kitchen, and a restroom with no flush toilet. This was the only place during our stay in Manchuria that did not have a flush toilet. We were lucky to have moved farther inland from the Siberian border, because in about a year, the Russians would invade Manchuko and overrun Hailar.

We used to go to school as a neighborhood group. When we saw a group of Manchurian kids, we exchanged provocative words. Korean kids came to the same school as the Japanese. They had Japanese names, and I was not aware that they were forced to have Japanese names. We could not distinguish the people of the two countries, and when they said they were Koreans, we asked them to speak some Korean. The Japanese spoke standard Japanese. We often had new arrivals from Japan; they usually spoke in dialects. I remember one from Okinawa; he had a distinctly different accent. His family may have come because Okinawa was getting too dangerous to live in. These Japanese may have come to Qiqihar to escape air raids by the Americans.

I had a classmate across the street in a two-story, four-unit apartment. On New Year's Day, 1945, this classmate wrote his New Year's Day wish on a Japanese paper with a brush. It was "必 勝," which means "Firm Conviction of Victory" in two Chinese characters. It is a Japanese custom to write a New Year's Day wish using a catchy phrase. The radio announcers told us often that the Japanese were to die fighting to the last person. My classmate may have firmly believed in the final victory. Almost every day, we heard over the radio about air raids over the Japanese cities by hundreds of B29s. However, Qiqihar was peaceful, and we went to school without concerns; we felt war was far away.

On August 8, 1945, as I was brushing my teeth, I heard over our radio that the Russians had invaded Manchuko, so we stopped going to school. I was in the sixth grade, the last year of Japanese primary school. We had air raids two or three times by a few Russian planes. We heard that they bombed the railroad station. My father's hotel was the upper floors of the station, but there was no obvious damage.

On August 6, just prior to the Russian invasion, we heard that a new type of bomb was dropped on Hiroshima, destroying the whole city. I distinctly remember the radio announcer saying it was an atomic bomb, and no vegetation would grow in that area for many years hence. However, I later learned that the people were not told it was an atomic bomb. It was obvious the Japanese were losing the war. However, they were saying they would fight to the last person, many with bamboo sticks. Many Japanese youth in Okinawa did that. Apparently, the Americans believed the Japanese would keep on fighting. Two atomic bombs were dropped in succession on Hiroshima and Nagasaki to destroy the Japanese will to fight to the end. A single B29 flew over each city and dropped the bomb. *Recently, I heard on a NHK TV program that a former pilot stationed near Nagasaki at that time said that the Japanese surveillance had observed strange activities on Tinian. There were only a few B29s on the island, and on that day a single plane flew over to Nagasaki. He said he could have shot it down, but no order came to attack the plane.*

We heard over the radio that hundreds of planes were coming almost every day to drop incendiary bombs on Japanese cities. More than sixty cities were burned; the worst one was Tokyo on March 10, 1945. *I remember the date because on that day in 1905, the Japanese Army had won the battle of Hoten (Shenyang) that induced the Russian Army to give up fighting.* The incendiary bombs were dropped in a large circle on wood and paper houses of ordinary Japanese civilians\; people inside the circle had no way to escape. *Later at the University of Washington, a student from Tokyo, who worked at my grandparents restaurant in Spokane prior to going to the University and who had become my friend, told me that there were blackened bodies stretched out like statues all over the area. Trucks came by to pick them up by shovels—more than one hundred thousand were killed. The Yoshiwadas, my youngest uncle's family, lived in a house that was a semi-Western style on the slope of a hill in Shibuya near the center of Tokyo. None of the houses around there were bombed. It was obvious that the bombs were aimed at wooden houses of defenseless citizens, who were trapped with no place to escape. Later, General Curtis LeMay who had instigated these bombings admitted that if America had lost the war, he would have been a war criminal for sure. These were poor people. Those who could afford to move out to the countryside, including my uncle's family, did as soon as there were possibilities of bombing. I think the Tokyo air raid was as bad as an atomic bomb.*

Many Japanese were moving in from Japan to Manchuko at that time thinking it was safer. Our next-door neighbor came from Japan just one day before the end of the war. Apparently they believed the Russians would honor the nonaggression treaty. *I heard many years later that the Japanese government had feelers out to Russia for her allies to end the war. I do not know why they trusted the Russians to transmit the message to the Americans and British. Recently, I learned also that the Russians were moving soldiers and weapons from the*

European front to the Manchurian border as rapidly as possible to invade Manchuria. They wanted to inflict as much damage as possible on the Japanese prior to their surrender to get even from the loss of the Russo-Japanese War. They fought the shortest time and were the only country that kept the Japanese islands—four islands east of Hokkaido. Even after more than seventy years, they have not returned those islands, claiming they are part of the Kuril Islands. Japan did not sign the peace treaty with Russia because of this issue.

At noon on August 15, we heard a special radio broadcast by the emperor stating the war had ended. For some reason many neighbors came to our house to listen. Many women were crying. I do not know whether they were crying because Japanese lost the war or because they were relieved the war was over—probably both. The Russian Army appeared a week or more later.

Therefore, it is not true that they overran Manchuko prior to the end of the war. Qiqihar was a major city in northern Manchuko and would have been a target. The book The Summer Russia Invaded Manchuria *(Handou, 2002), has a map showing the extent of the Russian invasion at the time of the Japanese surrender. According to the map, the Russians were nowhere near the railroad connecting Qiqihar, Harbin, Changchun, Shenyang, and Dalian.*

The refugees from Hailar came prior to the Russians—soon after the end of the war. We had four rooms. The chef of the Hailar Yamato Hotel had a family of four, and they were given the room with 4½ tatami mats.

Mrs. Iwaki, the wife of a soldier, with one daughter, who was about two years old, was given a room with 2½ tatami mats. I assumed her husband was a defender of Hailar fort and was probably taken to Siberia after the war. We slept in the room with six tatami mats. Each family had just enough space to spread a futon for each member of the family. Miss Nagata, a middle-aged lady, who used to be a maid of the Hasegawas in Dalian, was also a refugee from Hailar, and she slept in the room with eight tatami mats, which was the most spacious room; we used it as the family room for all the families. Miss Nagata had no privacy. After spending the winter with us, she left for Dalian. We do not know if she got there safely. *When we met the Hasegawas many years later, they did not seem to remember*. We had five large trunks in the living room full of goods from America. These were gradually sold as our source of income after the war.

At the beginning we had some food supplies from the Yamato Hotel, and the chef cooked for us a few times. The practice did not last very long, and soon the chef was earning some income by opening an eating-place by the roadside, using the remaining supplies.

I sold cigarettes made by Miss Nagata. It was just enough for my spending money. I roamed the city selling cigarettes and learned more about the city than I knew prior to the end of the war. I had been too busy studying during the war to venture around the city. My two sisters sold steamed corn bread they bought from a Chinese merchant. I do not think it amounted to much income either.

The chef from Hailar had two kids, a son and a daughter. His son was in about the fourth grade but was drinking shochu, a strong sake. The chef was a heavy drinker and often had fights with his wife. I heard his wife was a former geisha in Kyoto. When they had a fight, she usually threw him to the floor. One terrible event I could not forget was that she was pregnant. They aborted the baby at a late stage in the pregnancy. They left the baby in our family room on the top of a trunk. The baby cried for almost a week before it died. The mother was not permitted to go into the room; Ms. Nagata was probably gone by that time. Another death I remember, whose funeral I attended, was one of my classmates. He was a bully of the class. I still remember his death face—his nose holes plugged up with cottons.

Now, every time I see half-starved babies and little children in pictures from Africa on TV, it reminds me of that baby, and I think the chef made the right decision. Whenever I hear a plea from a speaker to help those hungry babies, I question why those parents have so many children when they know they have problems feeding them. I did ask one speaker about this. His reply was that they were not educated; educating those women would be the solution. I doubt educating women would solve over population and its consequences.

The Russian soldiers came into town wearing faded, dirty uniforms. The Japanese soldiers surrendered to them wearing new uniforms. If they had not been loaded onto trucks, they would have looked more like the victors. The Russians were uneducated and rude. We heard they were from Siberian prisons. They came into our house and took anything mechanical such as watches, clocks, and radios. They raped young women; so young women shaved their heads and wore men's clothing. The Russians used the Japanese men as laborers to carry away anything that was movable—from electric generators at the power plant to dried vegetables and fruits made for Japanese soldiers. The Russians even took grain hulls. Our father had a hernia, which was the reason he was not drafted into the Japanese Army. For some reason he had surgery on it just prior to the end of the war. Therefore, he was able to work as a laborer for the Russians.

The Russians cut off the city water supply and electricity as soon as they came. Our neighbors dug a well nearby. I remember the water was muddy; I do not remember how we used it. Perhaps it cleared up eventually. We lighted the family room with oil in an ashtray with a cotton wick sticking out. It created huge, dark shadows of each of us. It scared the little daughter of Mrs. Iwaki; she would cry and try to get away from it. The only way to stop her was for her mother to embrace her. *We did not know what happed to Mrs. Iwaki's husband. My mother exchanged letters with her for a while after going back to Japan. I do not think he came back alive.*

My sixth-grade teacher was drafted just prior to the end of the war, but I saw him selling his belongings on the roadside. At least he did not surrender to the Russians. Maybe local draftees were still in town and went home when the war was over.

The Russians took our doctors and engineers. By the end of the war, our mother's caries had moved to her chest. She was bedridden, and her doctor used to come with two nurses to take fluid out of her chest with a large syringe. Soon after the arrival of the Russians, her doctor disappeared, probably taken away to Siberia. Subsequently, only the nurses came.

We kept the house warm over the winter by getting coke from the nearby power plant, which we supplemented with coal that we bought occasionally. When we made the trip to the power plant the first time, Father did not have working clothes to wear. Until the end of the war, Father did not do anything around the house and did not have any clothes to wear to do chores. Therefore, he was wearing a Mantetsu uniform. A Russian soldier stopped my father as we headed to the power plant and forced him to trade his uniform with that of the solder's dirty uniform with holes. Subsequently, Father always wore the Russian uniform with leather patches covering the holes at the elbows and knees. It became Father's favorite work clothes. The uniform was so faded that others probably did not notice it was a Russian uniform. He wore it to do the forced labor for the Russians. I think he got the leather pieces from one of the places he worked for them. He also brought me back a new Japanese Army cap, which I wore to get cokes.

On New Year's Day 1946, Father wrote his wish: " 東 望," two Chinese characters meaning "aspire East." He probably meant going to Japan, *but as I reflect on that period, he may have thought of going all the way to*

27

America where our grandparents were probably worry-ing about us.

The Russian soldiers did not get along with the Chi-nese civilians. I saw Russian soldiers chasing after them and shooting at unarmed Chinese a couple of times. The Russians were gone almost as soon as they carried off all the movable things; I think they left sometime in the early spring.

The Nationalist Chinese Army then took over the city. By then the Chinese Nationalists were fighting against the Communists. The Nationalists had weapons from the United States including planes. The Communists were using weapons taken from the Japanese Army. Yet the Nationalists were losing the battles, and they did not stay very long in Qiqihar. *I learned later that the Russians were friendlier to the Nationalists than to the Commu-nists and stayed out of their civil war.*

One day before dawn, we heard gunshots from a distance. When we got up in the morning, we saw the Communist soldiers. I think it was late spring. To my surprise there were several Japanese soldiers among them. Soon thereafter, one of the Japanese soldiers came to our neighborhood gathering and gave us a talk about Communism. He told us the Communists are for com-mon people and that common people supported them. This was the reason they were winning the civil war even though the Nationalists were better equipped. He said Nationalists are for the rich and corrupt. He also said there were about fifty thousand Japanese soldiers in the Koanrei Mountains with food supplies sufficient to last for five years. *That sounded like a long time, but in retrospect five years passed by quickly, and I do not know what happened to them.*

The Communists' army was called "Paro-Gun" or the Eighth Army. It was the most famous unit of the Communists and was led by Lin Piao. They gave a rough time to the Japanese Army during the Pacific War. *Later in the Korean War, they were the soldiers who fought the Americans to a stalemate along the thirty-eighth parallel.*

Communist soldiers appeared friendly to us, but I was scared of them. One day while digging up coke at the power plant, one Japanese kid took my cap and placed it on the head of a soldier sitting by us. I was too scared to get it back. It also reminded me of a green and black beanie I had from America. I saw a baby wearing it, carried by his mother. I was certain I had the only beanie of that color in all of Manchuria. I did not know mine was missing; my father probably sold it as he had sold many of our belongings by the roadside. I was too shy to wear it and almost never did; the baby looked happy wearing it.

Soon after the Communists took control of the city, they subjected the Nationalists to the People's Court. A captor put several men and women on a horse-drawn carriage. Their hands had been tied at their backs and dunce caps placed on their heads. The captor whipped them as the carriage went around the city. He told the spectators that they were spies and enemies of the people. At the end they were shot to death. I watched one execution. A prisoner was told to walk away. As he walked the captor shot him from behind. I looked away at the instant he was shot. Next I saw a woman, probably his wife, crying beside him.

I usually roamed around the city alone, but sometimes I had a companion—Morita Shizuro. I will mention about our friendship during the evacuation, in the next chapter. Another friend I encountered was a former neighbor from Shenyang, Suzuki Manabu. One day he appeared near our home out of nowhere. We exchanged a few greetings, and then he disappeared. I never saw him again.

I attended an English class offered by a former teacher of Qiqihar Middle School at his home. There were only a few of us, and I do not remember how frequently we gathered. Prior to the evacuation, he gave us a certificate that stated we were students in the Qiqihar Middle School. After we settled in Japan, I used it to enroll in Hofu Middle School.

CHAPTER 5:
EVACUATION FROM MANCHURIA.

On September 12, 1946, the date etched in my memory, we were finally told to gather at the train station as neighborhood groups. More than one year after the war, we finally got a train to go to a port and get us out of Manchuria. We lived in several rows of duplex single-story houses or two-story buildings consisting of four units. Our row was duplex houses, and many of the units were accommodating refugees from Hailar like us. Each group was assigned to a boxcar. I do not remember interacting with anyone in the boxcar even though we knew each other. Our boxcar was full with no space to move around. A hole was made in a corner for a toilet— there was no privacy.

By the time of evacuation, we had nothing left to sell. There was no usable coke left at the power plant and not enough money to buy coal. If we had stayed over another winter, we would have all frozen to death. Someone told me that in a schoolyard in Shenyang there was a pile of dead bodies—people frozen to death during the first winter.

On the train each of us carried a sack full of food and some clothing. The food consisted of popped soybeans and diced millet cakes. A Chinese vendor sold slices from a steamed millet cake shaped like an upside down wok with a layer of red beans at its bottom. It was on a cart covered with a quilt to keep it warm. It had no taste but was a cheap way to fill one's stomach. A Chinese man at a roadside had a little spherical bomb to pop them over charcoal fire. All the vendors, Chinese selling produce and Japanese selling household goods, were by the roadside. I do not remember ever going into a building to buy something.

We made a prolonged stop in Shinkyo (Changchun), the former Capital of Manchuko, for at least a week. We stayed in an apartment of a former Japanese resident of the city and slept together under the one blanket we had. It was already too cold to sleep without it, and we needed each other for warmth. One night my father made us miso soup with uncut spinach in our dirty metal washbowl; it had scum stuck to the side of the bowl. It looked terrible, but it was the first warm dish we had since leaving Qiqihar.

I spent most of my time roaming around with Shizuro Morita, who appeared out of nowhere from another train every time our trains stopped. We had some spending money and used it to buy some sausages for ourselves. Morita was going back to Tachikawa near Tokyo. We exchanged our addresses, but I lost his, and I did not get a letter from him either.

The most dangerous situation we encountered was the crossing of a battlefield between the Chinese Nationalists and the Communists. The battle line was near Shiheigai (Siping) between Changchun and Shenyang. They apparently stopped fighting to let us walk through; we did not hear any gunshots, and there were no signs of soldiers anywhere. We hired a Chinese porter named Liu to carry our heaviest bag. The distance was estimated to be four ri, which is about ten miles. Mother barely made it, using Father's golf club as a stick. The rest of us carried whatever we could on our backs. My brother, Shogo, who was five years old at that time, carried a small backpack, too. The father of my classmate Fujita, who lived across the street, died during the walk. The Fujitas lost their mother soon after the war. She burned her foot walking over a boiling kettle on a shichirin, a small charcoal cooker; it induced tuberculosis. They were recent arrivals to Manchuria; so the Fujitas knew where to go in Japan without their parents.

I appreciated and respected the Chinese for not harassing us during the walk. Instead, they helped us, and we paid them in Manchuko currency, which would have been worthless, once we left Manchuria. For reasons I do not understand, Manchurians preferred this currency to the military currency of the Communists or Nationalists. I remember seeing posters along our path saying they hated Japanese fascists but not the Japanese people.

On the Communist side, we were in boxcars, but on the Nationalist side, we were in coal cars with a ridge at the middle and no roof. My sister Minako remembers that she got wet from rain, but I do not remember it. We had a short stop in Shenyang (September 30). Morita came again, but I saw him for the last time. In Shenyang we had to change to a lumber car with no sidewalls. The train moved slowly to Koroto (Huludao), where we boarded an American landing ship, tank (LST); it was October 11. We got a cabin because our father could work as an interpreter in the case that we encountered American soldiers. The rest of the Japanese were packed in the bottom of the boat. I stayed on the deck most of the time to avoid getting seasick. The Japanese cruiser Shira Yuki zoomed by us with a boat full of other evacuees.

It took us four days to get to Sasebo. A rusted, small aircraft carrier was in the bay; I did not know they could be so small. Mountains covered with green trees came right to the shore. It was a beautiful sight. I wrote a poem to reminisce the scene, in haiku format.

Sasebo Harbor
Rusty little carrier
By myriad of green.

We were subjected to showers of DDT. A Japanese American soldier was watching us. We were served huge sweet potatoes. It was a delicacy to us initially because there were no sweet potatoes in northern Manchuria, but we got tired of them quickly because they were tasteless and that was all we got to eat.

After a couple of days at Sasebo, we got on a train and traveled to Hofu; the city was never bombed. It was October 17, thirty-six days after we left Qiqihar. We walked to our uncle's home, which was about fifteen minutes away. Mother was barely walking, using Father's golf putter as a cane as we entered the front entrance. (I wish we'd kept the golf putter.) Aunt Asako and her eldest daughter, Toyoko, greeted us.

In retrospect the only thing I regret is that we forgot to bring back our photographs. They were hidden in a bamboo footlocker on the bottom level of the closet. In the back of the closet was a hole to escape to next door in case the Russians came into our house. They did come, and they took our radio, clocks, and watches, but we did not escape through the hole; we just watched.

According to the NHK TV program "Evacuation from Koroto (Hulutao)" shown on March 10, 2009, President Truman wanted the Japanese to be evacuated from Manchuria and the rest of China because the US government was afraid that these Japanese would be used by the Chinese Communists. Actually, both the Communists and Nationalists used the Japanese soldiers (John Dower, 2010). This corroborated my observation of a Japanese soldier in the Communist uniform mentioned previously. One hundred eighty-five LST ships were used; the first shipload departed from Hulutao on May 7, 1946. The official purpose was to ship the Nationalist Army into Manchuria and then use the same ships to send the Japanese to Japan and the Chinese in Japan to China. A little more than 1.05 million Japanese were evacuated out of more than 1.5 million Japanese that were present in Manchuria at the end of the war. About 250,000 died, and the rest remained in Manchuria to work for the Chinese government(s); most of them eventually returned to Japan.

The main evacuee shown on the program was a daughter of a kaitakudan farmer. (kaitakudans were sent by the Japanese government to establish farms, but actually, they took away the farms from the Manchurians at very low price and gave them to the Japanese farmers). She walked alone all the way from a town near her village in Northeast Manchuria to Shenyang and led about four hundred orphans back to Japan from Huludao in an earlier ship.

*The kaitakudan was an ill-conceived program by a section of the Japanese government with a backing of the Kwantung Army, and the first group was sent in 1933 (*Japan Chronik, *1991: 1062–1063). The army took away the farms from Manchurians mostly in the northeast section of Manchuko and gave them to the Japanese farmers. The primary purpose may have been to secure the region from Chinese warlords for the possible invasion of Siberia. This is suggested by the requirement that these farmers were healthy young men between the ages of seventeen and forty-five. Japanese farmers were very reluctant to go, but by the end of the war, there were 270,000 of them. However, these young men were drafted into the army, leaving behind women and children. Therefore, the Manchurians were justified immediately after the Japanese defeat to drive these Japanese out.*

36

Many died from cold, starvation, and suicide. As the NHK program showed, many children were left behind and adopted by the Manchurians. When these children grew up, many went to Japan to search for their parents and relatives, mostly without success. Japanese media covered these tragic stories, but I have not heard of any reports that criticized the Kwantung Army or the program that promoted emigration of the farmers. The Japanese civilians, including us, who had stayed put in their residences got out safely.

CHAPTER 6:
HOFU

Our uncle's house was a traditional style Japanese house, previously owned by General Kodama, a hero of the Russo-Japanese war (1904–1905)(personal communication, Yukio Kamada my cousin). He was considered the brain behind the Japanese Army that conquered Port Author and won the battle of Hoten (Shenyang). The house was big with many rooms and on a large lot. Uncle Toshisaku, who had inherited the family miso/soy sauce business, took his father's name, Hisanosuke, a common Japanese custom. He bought the house as the retirement home for his parents. We were given the tearoom, which faced the beautiful inner garden.

We resumed schooling. I was placed in the first-year class of Hofu Middle School, in the same building my father attended as a middle school student. The building was the same one-story, wooden structure, and the roof tiles were from the company owned by my grandmother's family. The company went bankrupt many years prior to the war. I had been away from the school for more than a year, except for occasional English lessons I had from a Qiqihar Middle School teacher. My Hofu classmates were learning physics, biology, algebra, English, and Japanese literature. Perhaps because of the English lessons I had, the only subject I understood well enough to get good grades in was English. My mother did not help me at all in English. She lay in bed most of the time. I remember my aunt said to me that unless I did better in school, I would bring shame to our family name. All her children were honor students; there were four of them in the school at that time.

Father worked for the Australian occupation force as office staff, utilizing his knowledge of English. He occasionally brought home edges of bread slices with butter on them. I thought they were leftovers, but in retrospect I do not think so. *I have never seen, even in America, people eating just the middle of a slice of bread buttered to the edge. I think our father purposely put lots of butter on the edges and brought them home for us hungry children. If he had brought whole slices of bread, his supervisor would not have permitted it.* We read in newspapers, occasionally, that people starved to death.

We ate better than the average Japanese did. We went occasionally to our grandfather's family farm in Yamaguchi city. I think our grandparents bought some additional farmland for the family prior to the war, and after the MacArthur reform, grandparents' farms were transferred probably to the grandfather's siblings. We got rice and vegetables from them. We called that rice "silver rice" and shared with our uncle's family. Hofu and Yamaguchi City were never bombed.

The Kawamura family owned a miso (soybean paste) and soy sauce company called Kanaya, but my uncle worked at a cement company in Ube, a nearby town. Yasui, the family of the oldest sister of my grandmother, operated the shop. We used to go there often to eat kouji, malted rice, which is an ingredient of the miso manufacturing process.

We played with our cousins that were close to our ages and a child of a family living in a separate house on the property. I learned to swim at nearby Sabagawa, a little river. I went deeper gradually until my hands were not touching the bottom and did the dog paddle to swim. I had access to a public swimming pool in Shenyang, but none of the other cities we lived in had one. Therefore, Sabagawa was the first chance I had to swim since Shenyang.

At Hofu Middle School during our ten minute recesses, we often played baseball with a soft tennis ball. A pitcher had an advantage over the batters because the ball could be squeezed causing sharp curves. My close friend Satoshi Kanazawa was usually the pitcher. In retrospect it was unbelievable that we played baseball between classes when we had less than ten minutes to play.

Kanazawa and I used to walk home together. He lived in a mountain village nearby. He was impressed by the appearance of our home; he thought some famous family lived there. It had a long, white wall with red stripes as camouflage against air raids. Another friend Hatsunori Sasaki sat behind me in the classroom. Both of them became my lifelong friends.

CHAPTER 7:
RETURNING TO THE UNITED STATES

Back in the States, our grandparents got out of the camp as soon as they learned they could as long as they did not go back to the Pacific Coast. They settled in Spokane, Washington, and started a restaurant at the front of Milwaukee Road Station called Ritz Café. They had Japanese cooks and served ordinary American dishes not Japanese dishes, but they also had some common Americanized Chinese dishes. Entrées on their menu were large but there was a special for each day of the week. I remember the Sunday special was chicken fricassee. *I realized, subsequently, that this and many other dishes were Southern dishes such as oxtail stew, pig hock, boiled beef heart, and corn bread. My favorites, which I still make sometimes, were spareribs and sauerkraut, corn beef and cabbage, and oxtail stew. If I find it* *in a market, I'll buy beef tongue, pigs' feet, and any other unusual parts. I cook all of these in a Crock-pot.*

Soon after our arrival in Hofu, our grandparents found us living at our uncle's house. They sent us care packages, but very often the contents were stolen—we received empty chocolate boxes but got powdered eggs. They soon started the processes of getting us back to the States.

After about a fourteen-month stay in Hofu, our mother and we four children got the permit to go back to the States, but our father could not go back because he did not have an American citizenship (the reason we left the States back in 1939). *Father decided to send us back probably because he thought we would have better life in America than in Japan where we had to struggle to find enough food to eat.*

Photo 7: The family photo prior to leaving for America, leaving Father behind. The front row left to right: Minako, Mother, Shogo, Yoko, Father. At the center: Kanji.

On the way to Tokyo, we saw from the train station a glimpse of Hiroshima ruined by the atomic bomb. *Many years later I went to its museum and remember bones imbedded in concrete. The temperature must have been so hot around the epicenter that fleshes were burned instantly and bones were imbedded in melted concrete.*

We stayed for about a month in Shibuya, Tokyo, with Uncle Yoshiwada's family while we were finishing up the paper work to go to America. They lived in a traditional Japanese house saved from the fire of the air raids probably because it was on the slope of a hill. *Many years later we learned that they were evacuated out into the countryside and came back just prior to our stay with them.*

The Yoshiwadas had five children. Hideko was the eldest, one year older than I. Etsuko was one year younger than I. Their eldest son, Tetsuo, was about June Minako's age, and Yasusuke was about Irene Yoko's age. Tamiko, the youngest, was only about two years old.

I went around with Hideko san and Etsuko san; they took me to Ginza. Many Ginza buildings were destroyed by air raids; those that remained, such as a department store, were taken over by the American occupation force. The stores were under temporary structures along both sides of the road. It was the Christmas season, and Hideko and Etsuko sang "Silent Night Holy Night" frequently, even though they were not Christians. That was the first time in my memory I'd heard that hymn. Until I met Etsuko san, I never felt an attraction toward a female. I felt she was the most beautiful gentle girl I'd ever met. She usually had on a sweater of a pinkish color mixed in with cream color. The sweater was soft, and I

45

frequently lay my head on her arm. It felt good, and she did not object.

We went to Yokohama Harbor on January 7, 1948. As the ship left port, we watched Father and the Yoshiwada family standing on the pier until they became invisible to us. I was on deck admiring the majestic, purple Mount Fuji until it sank below the horizon. That beautiful scenery is etched in my memory forever.

Oh Fuji, Fuji

Majestic, purple

Sinking beyond horizon as the sun rises

The ship was the General Meigs. It was used as a military transport and was not yet converted back completely to a passenger ship; it still had bunk beds even though we were in first-class cabins. Male and female passengers were segregated. I shared a cabin with three other guys. One had survived the atomic bomb in Hiroshima because his house collapsed above him. The only other thing I remember was that when I woke up, I was embracing my pillow, dreaming of Etsuko san. She was my first love.

That was the fourth and last time we crossed the Pacific on a ship and the only time I remember. We arrived on January 17 in San Francisco. Our grandparents came from Spokane to San Francisco in a rented Cadillac with a hired taxi driver, who was a regular customer at the Ritz Cafe. The place we came back to was Opportunity, Washington, a suburb of Spokane.

It was really the land of opportunity for us, their grandchildren. Kanji, Minako, Yoko, and Shogo were dead as Japanese and reborn as Robert, June, Irene, and Jerry, respectively, to our second lives as Americans, full of hope and regaining our will to live. We enrolled at Opportunity Grade School from the beginning of the second semester on February 2, 1948.

CHAPTER 8:
REVISITING MANCHURIA

I n 2007 my sister Irene Yoko, my brother Jerry Shogo, and I revisited the cities where we used to live in
Manchuria (1939–1946). My other sister, June Minako,
refused to go because she did not want to recollect the
terrible experiences she had. My wife, Shigeko; her
cousin Sadakazu Hasegawa, who used to live in Dalian
(chapter 2), and his wife, Hisako; and my two cousins
Yukio Kamada and Hideko Suzuki (Yoshiwada, chapter 7) joined this tour, June 25 to July 2. Yukio found
a tour group to Manchuria, which planned to visit old
battlegrounds in the area. We negotiated with the director of the tour for us to join the group but to split off from
Hailar, and went on to Shenyang, Qiqihar, plus Dalian
where we visited Hasegawas prior to the war.

The cities described below are from my recollections
during this trip.

8-1 Shenyang

We lived in Hoten, present name Shenyang, from 1939 to 1943.

My father worked at the Hoten Yamato Hotel from 1939 to 1941. A Japanese architect designed the hotel, and the Japanese built it in 1927. It is one of the buildings on the circumference of the circle. All the buildings around the circle were built by the Japanese and are still in use. Now, much taller buildings surround the hotel, which was three stories high; Holiday Inn in the background dwarfs the hotel. We stayed in the hotel; it was maintained very well, and the marbled floor of the lobby still looked nice.

The street that goes off from the circle adjacent to Yamato Hotel leads to our former residential area and to Aoi Grade School where my sister June Minako and I used to go. In photo 8-1 I am standing at the front of the school, which is now a middle school. The building is

Photo 8-1: Former Aoi grade school

the same but the front entrance modified. We were not permitted to go into the building; the classes were in session.

We then went to Naganuma Park. It used to be an undeveloped little lake where we went for a picnic several times. Now, it is a well-developed lake with high-rise buildings in the background. A couple of boats with tourists were floating by as we watched. The population of the city used to be 1.3 million, and now it is 7.2 million. The guide told us that many of the high rises are apartments or condominiums owned by the government and leased to individual households on a seventy-year lease. The elevators are for people living on the eighth floor and up.

The former Mantetsu Hospital, where Jerry Shogo was born in 1941 is still used as a hospital. It is almost across the street from the back of the Yamato Hotel.

8-2 Hailar

Hailar is in Inner Mongolia in the midst of the prairie east of Gobi Desert. I remember the plain around Hailar as sandy desert, but now it is green prairies perhaps because we visited in early summer. The guide took us to the prairie near Hailar River where I remember fishing a couple of times. When we lived there, from 1943 to 1944, the streets were unpaved, and camels and Mongolians in their native customs were on the streets. We learned from the Hailar Museum guide in a native costume that the native people are not Mongolian but Urbenku, and they established Hailar more than one thousand years ago. They did not have the written form of their language and learned to write in Chinese only recently.

The streets are now paved and have cars and bicycles; they look like a street in downtown Spokane. The traffic was not as bad as in other cities we visited, but drivers were just as bad; they ignored pedestrians even on crosswalks. The air was dry and comfortable. The population is about two hundred thousand—it used to be about forty thousand. Now the Chinese make up most of the population.

We used to live in a Russian built house with rock siding. These houses and the Yamato Hotel no longer exist. The only things I recognized, walking around the former Japanese section, were the rocks from the walls of former houses; they were now being used as the foundation for the houses. Apparently, they were built soon after the war. These houses were already dilapidated and being removed.

8-3 Qiqihar

The Qiqihar Station was just as I remembered (photo 8-2). The upper floors were formerly Yamato Hotel where my father was the manager for about a year, until the end of the war when Mantetsu ceased to exist. Now the upper floors

Photo 8-2: Qiqihar Railroad Station

are the railroad company offices. We observed the hotel from the parking lot where we had gathered for the evacuation in September of 1946 (chapter 5).

We went to the place where the Japanese apartments used to be standing in rows of one- and two-story buildings. Now, many high-rise apartments occupied the area.

8-4 Dalian

Prior to the Pearl Harbor attack, we visited the Hasegawa house in Dalian (chapter 2). The house was on the slope of a hill, white and beautiful, and the inside had Western style rooms and furniture. My father lived there while looking for a job. Sadakazu was born in Dalian and lived in that house for about twenty years with his parents and two older sisters. He was glad that he was able to see it again. The house was about to be demolished. When we visited, it was the office to manage high-rise nursing homes nearby, and this house was the last of the residential houses remaining in the area. Sadakazu Hasegawa and his wife decided to join our trip at the last moment because their planned trip was canceled. We felt it was a miracle that we were able to see the house again.

CHAPTER 9:
RELEVANCE TO THE HISTORY OF MANCHUKO

My recollection as we revisited these sites was integrated with the historical facts (*Japan Chronik*, 1991).

Manchu established the Qing dynasty in 1644 with Shenyang as its capital; it was the capital for the first two emperors. The third emperor conquered the whole China and moved the capital to Beijing. We visited the Manchu palace of the initial phase of the Qing dynasty. The open court at the front of the emperor's palace was lined on both sides by the houses belonging to the leaders of the eight ethnic tribes of Manchuria, four houses on each side. I was not aware until then that Manchu consisted of so many tribes.

Russia had control of Manchuria by the beginning of the twentieth century, and she was threatening to control

Korea. The Japanese felt that unless they stopped the Russian advance prior to the Russian control of Korea, Japan would be colonized. The British and Americans did not like the Russian encroachment either. The British and the Japanese formed an alliance so that the combined forces could withstand the Russian threat.

After a series of negotiations to make the Russians withdraw from North Korea failed, Japan initiated the attack and declared war on Russia (February 8, 1904). The fiercest battle was fought to capture Height 203 overlooking Port Arthur, the home of the Russian Pacific fleet. By the time the Japanese attacked Height 203, the area was heavily fortified. The Japanese brought in heavy cannons that were used to protect a Japanese port from invaders. The cannons were effective in destroying Russian forts. We saw the monument still standing at Height 203. There were many tourists; apparently the Chinese are interested in the battle. After heavy casualties the Japanese Army defeated the Russian defenders, and the Russian commander signed the treaty to hand over the fort at Suishiei, the navy battalion interview station. Guns from Height 203 destroyed the Russian Pacific fleet after old ships were sunken to seal the port. The Japanese Army then advanced northward and defeated the Russians at the battle of Hoten (Shenyang) on March 10, 1905. However, the army could not advance any farther; their supplies were depleted.

The Russian Baltic fleet came after a long voyage. The Japanese Navy was waiting for them as they came to the Straight of Tsushima and destroyed them at the battle of the Japan Sea on May 27, 1905. It was a complete victory with hardly any loss on the Japanese side. Togo Heihachiro, the admiral of the combined fleet, was the most famous hero among many heroes of the war.

President Theodore Roosevelt intervened to stop the war; he received a Nobel Peace Prize for his work. A former Japanese classmate of Roosevelt at Harvard had a prior agreement with the president that at an appropriate moment, he would intervene to stop the war. Therefore, diplomacy was the important factor in the Japanese victory, but the Japanese were taught in schools that the victory was by Yamato Damashii, the Japanese spirit. They could defeat superior enemies by Yamato Damashii with poorer weapons. The Japanese military and citizens believed they could not be defeated. Japanese militarism started from the teaching about the Russo-Japanese War.

In China the major rebellion against the imperial rule of the Qing dynasty was started by the Taiping (Great Peace) Rebellion led by Hong Xiuquan in mid-nineteenth century. It initiated as a religious movement influenced by Protestant Christianity but became a popular uprising that took the Qing army fourteen years to squash (Reilly, 2010). The idea lived on, and finally, in 1912, Sun Yat-sen led the revolt and displaced the Qing dynasty and established the Republic of China and forced abdication of the Emperor Pu-Yi, ending the Qing dynasty. General Yuan Shikai became the president of the republic, but he did not have the control over Manchuria.

Manchuria was under the control of the warlord Zhang Zuolin. He was killed by the Kwantung Army, which controlled the railroad (1928). I remember going to his tomb site, climbing many steps at a hill, on an excursion trip from Aoi Grade School (circa 1941). His son, Zhang Xueliang, took over the control of Manchuria. Zhang Xueliang was a better politician and recognized as the ruler of Manchuria by the Republic of China.

The Manchu Incident occurred on September 18, 1931. It started when a unit of the Kwantung Army blew up a railroad northeast of Shenyang (Ryujouko) and blamed it on the Chinese Army. By the Manchu Incident, Zhang's army was driven out to North China by the Japanese Kwantung Army. When we visited the monument to the Manchu Incident, I learned that the Chinese consider that incident as the beginning of the fourteen-year Chinese-Japanese War that ended in 1945.

This incident led to the occupation of the whole Manchuria by the Kwantung Army, and the Japanese established the puppet state of Manchuko in 1932. Pu-Yi, the last emperor of the Qing dynasty, was enthroned as the emperor of the country in 1934.

Near the end of World War II, the Russians invaded Manchuria all along the Siberia-Manchuria border (August 8, 1945). Hailar was surrounded by an underground fort; the Hailar fort was the only place the whole tour group visited. One of the members was a former defender of Hailar fort. He told us that the Japanese defended the fort surrounding Hailar until many days after the war. Maybe that was the reason Qiqihar was not occupied until about a week after the war. The Japanese military tactic was to leave those defending the forts behind and for the rest of the army to retreat to the Korean border to defend Korea so that the Russians could not easily invade Japan.

All the defenders of the forts along the border with Siberia used the same tactic as the defenders of the islands in the Pacific. They fought until they were completely defeated and the leader of a fort or island committed suicide by hara-kiri. The defenders fought even after there was no chance that they could win, rather than surrender. *I realized that this custom came from the feudal period in the battles between the feudal lords. They did not surrender, and when they could no longer defend a castle against the attacking force, the commander committed suicide by hara-kiri as the castle burned.*

Manchuko ceased its existence as a country the instant Japan surrendered; this showed that Manchuko was a puppet country and could not have existed independent of Japan. She had her own emperor, a government with a Manchu prime minister, and her own army, but the inhabitants were not conscious that it was an independent country. The Japanese in Manchuko did not consider themselves citizens of Manchuko, but of Japan. They were not aware that the main part of the Kwantung Army had abandoned Manchuko and tactically retreated to the Korean border to defend Japan. The army was a part of the Japanese Army, and its duty was to defend the Japanese emperor, not his subjects in Manchuria. When the emperor of Japan ordered the Japanese to cease fighting, they did and surrendered to the Russians or the Chinese. The Manchurian Army disappeared.

The Japanese empire collapsed in a single broadcast by her emperor. It is amazing that when the emperor ordered the soldiers to quit fighting and throw down arms, those who heard him did. However, some soldiers that did not hear him kept on hiding in caves and jungles.

PART II:

A JAPANESE STUDENT IN AMERICAN SCHOOLS

CHAPTER 10:
OPPORTUNITY, WASHINGTON (1948–1952)

We started to go to the Japanese Methodist Church as soon as we settled in Opportunity (the only Japanese Christian church in Spokane was Methodist); our grandparents made us go there probably from the first Sunday. The minister of the church, Rev. Taro Goto, and his wife, Alice, were close friends of our grandparents. Mrs. Goto had accompanied our grandparents to San Francisco to pick us up. They had two sons, one my age and another around my sister Irene's age. We went to the parish prior to the service and read the Sunday comics section. We were told that it was the best way to learn English. *I did not get out of this habit until my kids started to read the comics; I thought I was setting a bad example.* About a year later, Reverend Goto became the superintendent of the whole Japanese West Coast Conference and moved to Sacramento with his family.

I remember the first day at the Opportunity Grade School very well; it was the first day of second semester. I was placed in the eighth grade in a class made up of seventh and eighth grade students. The second year in a Japanese middle school is the same year as eighth grade in America except the American school system starts a half-year earlier. I had learned some English in Japan. Therefore, they thought I should be able to keep up with the eighth grade students. However, my sisters did not have any English; so June was placed in the second grade and Irene in first. They were sixth and fourth grade, respectively, in Japan. Mrs. Coddington, a friend of Alice Goto, took us to the school. She knew Janet Mudgett in my class, apparently from Spokane Valley Methodist Church. She was a blond with a nice figure. I thought she was the most beautiful girl I had ever seen. The girl in my dream switched from Etsuko to Janet. She and Bobby Ford were very helpful during my eighth grade year. All the girls in the class were already using red lipstick, and they were very expressive when they talked. I thought I was watching movie actors and felt very shy and nervous when they tried to talk to me.

Mathematics and science were easy. In Japan I was learning algebra, biology, and physical sciences. In eighth grade they were still studying arithmetic and general science. I was too shy to speak English, but I soon found out I knew enough English grammar to get an A in the class.

Mr. Meyer was the teacher. He was a little tense but a very kind teacher. He shocked me by sitting on a pile of books on his desk to talk to us. In Japan we were taught to respect books and never to sit on them. Another difference in manners was students smoking in front of the principal; in Japan we would be kicked out of school, even when we were caught smoking off school grounds.

One incident I remember was that I took a test on something. I wrote the answers in Japanese thinking I would translate them later. However, there was not enough time at the end, so I handed it in as it was. He gave me an A saying that the answers must be correct even though he could not read them. I hardly had any problems understanding what we were taught and graduated from grade school with the rest of the eighth grade at the end of the semester.

Starting in the fall of 1948, I began attending Central Valley High School at Greenacres, Washington, near the Idaho border. I took all the science and mathematics courses that were offered because I thought if I was spending time studying, I might as well learn something concrete. I was not aware of how well I was doing academically. Often, I was the only one that finished assignments. In my sophomore year, I was one of only two who were elected to the National Honor Society. That made me realize I was near the top of the class scholastically. I ended up valedictorian of the class (120 students) and gave a speech at the commencement exercise, the first public speech I had ever made. Judging from the newspaper article the next morning, I doubt that the audience understood what I said. I said commencement means the beginning, the beginning of our lives independent of our parents. Rev. Shigeo Shimada of Highland Park Methodist Church, the Spokane Japanese Church, attended the graduation as my Father substitute.

I remember learning from Coach Sig Hanson, our football coach, in his civics class the essence of American democracy. Majority rules but protects minorities and the disadvantaged. *I regretted to learn that by the time my children went to school, civics was no longer taught.* Mrs. Eastburn was the excellent mathematics and Latin teacher; in her last lesson, she gave me a worn-out algebra textbook without a cover, which I do not remember ever using, but *I still had it in September of 2000 when I wrote the first draft of this section.* Mr. Muse was a friendly science teacher from whom I learned chemistry and physics. With his encouragement I submitted an essay on the origin of the universe to the Westinghouse scholarship contest. I do not have a copy of it, but in retrospect I suspect that it was written in terrible English. I doubt that the selection committee members ever read the proposal.

Later, at the University of Washington, I had to take tests to determine my placement level in classes in mathematics and general chemistry. I was near the top in mathematics, and I was admitted to the advanced class of general chemistry. I did not consider Central Valley to be an academic high school. Therefore, I was surprised and happy to be at the top level on these subjects. Only three of us from my graduating class went to the University of Washington. Many years later, at a class reunion, I learned that most of those who went to college went to Washington State or technical schools.

During my senior year, I was nominated by Janet Mudget as the student body vice president and was elected. I consider it an honorary position. I did nothing during the tenure. At one student council meeting, Roy Shaw, the president, was late showing up. I was asked to preside, but I refused.

I was only an average student in the Japanese schools. At Central Valley I had to study from textbooks because I did not understand what teachers were saying most of the time. Therefore, I was the only one who did assignments regularly. The self-study became my way to learn and solve problems. This may be the most worthwhile habit I picked up during my high school years, and it gave me self-confidence. However, this may be the reason I have my own way to pronounce some words, which when said nobody understands.

I usually walked between home and Opportunity Grade School and went to the high school from there on a school bus. The walking distance was about ten minutes, and several of us walked in the same direction, but as my classmates reminded me at subsequent class reunions, I did not talk much. Janet Mudget walked in the same direction occasionally, but I was infatuated with her and afraid; I kept a distance. A classmate noticed this and teased me about it.

During my senior year, Jerry Drinkard gave Gordon Peterson and me a ride in his Model A Ford to school frequently. We also went to movies and drive-ins several times. Gordon and I developed a lasting friendship. We interact to this day; he is the reason I started going to the class reunions, probably from the thirty-fifth reunion, and I usually stayed at his house when he lived in Spokane. Subsequently, he got a farm by the Columbia River with a hill on the property. Both my wife and I stayed there a couple of times.

Whenever I went to our class reunions, I was usually asked to give a speech. I talked about my high school and lifetime experiences. I considered my talks to partially make up for my silence during the high school years. The organizing committee told us that the fiftieth reunion was our last meeting but that we might have mini-reunions. However, we still had the reunions as big as the former ones and more frequently, every two years instead of every five years. As I was finishing the final revision of this manuscript, we had our sixtieth. The organizing committee members were almost the same each time except for the host. I went to one in Port Angeles hosted by Spencer Flegel and another near Ocean City hosted by Gene Schermer. Both have very nice homes near the ocean. The classmates that showed up at the reunions all had successful lives and now live happily in retirement.

CHAPTER 11:
UNIVERSITY OF WASHINGTON (1952–1956)

I was set to go to Gonzaga University. However, I received a scholarship from Standard Oil Company to attend the University of Washington. I did not apply for any scholarships; it was god sent. *I became aware that every time I had to make a life-altering decision, the most appropriate opportunity came to me.* I only had to accept it. The scholarship was only $500 and for one year, but it was sufficient for me to go to the top school in the state. The tuition was $55 per quarter, and the room and board at a student co-op was $150 a quarter. These expenses remained constant throughout the time I was at the university. My grandmother wanted me to be an MD, so I enrolled as a premed student.

Grandmother took me to Seattle and to St. Peter's Episcopal Church, a Japanese church, where my
grandparents were members from the beginning of the
church. She introduced me to Reverend Shoji, the first
pastor of the church, and many of her old friends. They
all knew me, but I did not remember even one of them.
Reverend Shoji's family and Yoshida's family, my grandparents' old friends, invited me for dinner several times
while I attended the university. I attended St. Peter's
Church several times but did not participate in the Holy
Communion, which was for the members only. Sometimes I attended University Temple Methodist Church,
adjacent to the campus, but did not become a member.
I attended several other churches including a Buddhist
church once. I could not understand a single word from
the Buddhist prayer book, which they chanted during
their worship service. I felt others in the congregation
did not understand either. I never went back to the Buddhist church but read books about them.

My grandparents sold their home in Opportunity soon
after I left for Seattle. My mother and siblings moved
to Seattle soon after. When they moved I lost several of
my belongings including my high school class annuals,
except one survived by chance, the one from my junior
year. I feel the lamp stand Grandfather made out of driftwood while they were at Minidoka was the most important irreplaceable item that got lost.

A large oil painting of a fuji lady [a lady clad in a kimono with a picture of fuji (wisteria) flowers] painted by
my former art teacher at Hofu Middle School was also

lost, probably stolen. I requested it by Grandmother's wish. Grandmother promised to send him a suit as the payment but did not keep her promise. Many years later, I met him; he remembered the painting, and I felt bad (chapter 15).

Every vacation I went back to Spokane to help my grandparents with their hotel and restaurant. I was up by six in the morning and went to bed after midnight. I was so sleepy in the morning that I mopped the front lobby half-asleep, bumping into the coal stove in the middle of the lobby almost every morning. The hotel, Great Northern Hotel, was at the edge of skid row across the street from the Milwaukee Road Station. The customers were mostly transient laborers, winos, and some retired persons. The rooms were from fifty cents to a dollar. The retired person had a room for fourteen dollars a month. The guests were all men. When, once in a while, a white woman came up the stairs to the registration desk, a police detective appeared almost instantly and led her away. They did not care if an American Indian woman came up. Except for our family members and employees, none of the Asian women ever came up. At the restaurant, Ritz Café, I was a cashier, waiter, dishwasher, and sometimes even a fry cook. I received fifty dollars a week working for my grandparents; it was sufficient pay for me to be able to go to the university.

When I got back to the university, I was so tired that I slept through many lectures. I remember in a mathematics class a student sitting next to me wondered how I could get As in exams while I was sleeping most of the time. My mother gave me a Parker fountain pen, which I used to write lecture notes. The lecture halls for introductory courses were large with concrete floors. I was so sleepy during the lectures that I dropped the pen frequently; the pen did not last long. Once, I picked up a sack lunch belonging to a person sitting next to me, by mistake. I felt embarrassed and threw it in a garbage can.

One funny incident that showed my ignorance of social etiquette was that I was invited to an informal luncheon at the Washington Athletic Club, which was held for the recipients of Standard Oil Company scholarships. I thought "informal" meant ordinary day clothes. I went wearing a leather jacket, and I had to go back to my room and change to a tie and a sport jacket. Until then I did not know that informal meant a tie and a jacket. I learned that I was selected for the scholarship as one of leaders for tomorrow (1952–1953).

The student co-op house I stayed in was the McGregor House. We had an honorary housemother, and the house was named after her. She came for Sunday dinner occasionally. The house was about five blocks away from the campus near the far end of the Greek houses, on the last street before the cliff.

The co-op had a central kitchen, and food was delivered to us for dinner. We took turns serving and washing dishes. We also made breakfasts. One of the residents was from Formosa, and he made eggs looking like overcooked pancakes. Some of the residents thought I had made them. I felt insulted because I had experience as a fry cook. However, I kept quiet; I was still very shy.

Most of us slept in a large room on the ground floor with rows of bunk beds. Most of the windows were broken, and the door to outside was usually wide open. It got cold in winters, especially on windy nights. Some of us stayed there throughout the time we were students. I stayed there until I graduated, but eventually I moved up to sleep in my own room where it was warm.

Many years later, there was a movie called Animal House. That house at Harvard was just like ours. Our house was just as dilapidated as the Animal House, and college life was just like that in the movie. I remember almost every time after final exams many house members celebrated by getting drunk; a few of them passed out along the sidewalk in front of the house and in hallways inside. I did not drink during the college days.

The historical event in biological science occurred in the spring quarter while I was a freshman, and I was not aware of it. James Watson and Francis Crick proposed that DNA is a double helix and probably duplicates using each strand as the template (Nature, 1953). I was taking a general biology course from a textbook that did not have a single entry about DNA. The professor who taught the class did not mention the paper; he should have told us of its significance. It was the fundamental discovery in molecular biology; subsequent research in the field is based on it. I did not dream that the mechanisms of its replication would become my research project during the prime of my research career.

At the end of my sophomore year, I went for an interview at the University of Washington School of

Medicine. I was asked why I want to be an MD. I said I want to do medical research. I was told that it is unnecessary to get an MD to do research, and it is difficult for a minority to establish a medical practice. I was shocked when told that the motive for going to medical school should be to make money. I was not interested in making money. I gladly changed my major to chemistry and told my grandmother. She did not object.

During the second semester of my senior year, I was doing a special project for physical chemistry laboratory. One day the professor in charge, Dr. B. Seymour Rabinovitch, came to my laboratory bench and asked me what my plan was for the future. I said I wanted to do research. He told me I needed to go to a graduate school, and I needed to apply immediately, or it would be too late. He took me to the chairman of the department, Dr. Paul C. Cross. I told Professor Cross that I was interested in thermodynamics. He told me that for that area of study, the University of Wisconsin was right for me. He was a graduate of Wisconsin. Soon after that, Dr. Irvine Shane from the Department of Chemistry at the University of Wisconsin came for a visit, and he offered me a teaching assistantship in his instrumental analysis class. Dr. Shane was a graduate of the University of Washington and was an assistant professor in analytical chemistry. *Many years later he served as the chancellor of the University of Wisconsin-Madison.* In 1956 I graduated cum laude with a BS in chemistry, looking forward to going to graduate school in Madison, Wisconsin.

That summer of 1956 Father finally came from Japan, almost nine years after our separation. He was not able to pay for his plane fare, and my grandparents were not doing well in their businesses and could not afford it. Therefore, I paid for it, even though I was just a poor student. Father arrived in Spokane only two weeks before I left for Madison. After nine years we had only a very short time together. He was gone during the most important period of my student life. His contribution to my life and to my two sisters and brother was insignificant. My siblings felt they did not know him.

During the time he was living by himself, Father was living near his older brother, Setsuzo Kawamura's home in Fujinomiya, Shizuoka Prefecture, and taught English and sociology at Fujinomiya East High School (1950-1956). Almost immediately after we left him, he went to Tokyo to live with the family of his younger brother, Motosuke Yoshiwada, and worked as a supreme translator of civilian affairs at the General Headquarters of the American occupational force until it was disbanded in 1949. One day soon afterward, Father met Uncle Setsuzo at a railroad station, and Uncle Setsuzo asked him to come to his home in Fujinomiya. He got the teaching position at the Fujinomiya East High School and taught there until he joined us. *In retrospect I think he enjoyed his life as a teacher the most. He was very popular among his students.*

By the time Father came, mother had divorced him and was living in Seattle with my siblings. I visited them occasionally on weekends. My sister June went to the University of Washington while I was in my senior year. I was not aware that my mother and siblings were struggling to make ends meet. I may have been the most well-to-do financially.

CHAPTER 12:
UNIVERSITY OF WISCONSIN-MADISON (1956–1961)

I went to Madison on a Greyhound bus; it took about thirty-nine hours. I was so tired and bored that I never took a bus again. I took trains back to Spokane and Seattle about once a year.

I found a room for five dollars a week near Vilas Park and found a family restaurant just like my grandparent's restaurant at a midpoint between my laboratory and my residence. They served about the same kind of food as the Ritz Café. I got meal tickets and ate dinners there regularly; I felt at home there.

I became a teaching assistant for instrumental analysis with Robert C. Hansen. I was still very shy and did not speak much. Bob did most of the talking. He became a close friend, and we moved into an apartment during the second semester. It was by the Enzyme Institute, very close to the Biochemistry Department. We lived together for about a year until he got married.

I was impressed by the systematic way he searched for a wife. He would call up a girl from his list every Wednesday for a date on Saturday night. He came back from a date and reported to me the behavior of his date. He was usually critical; he would say she drinks too much, talks too much, was too aggressive, etc. One day he came back and said that he found the girl he likes. He had a date with her at a dance at the YWCA. She did not drink or smoke. She was willing to live on a farm and can vegetables. Bob grew up on a farm near Eau Claire, Wisconsin. His dream was to become a professor in a small college and have a small farm. He attained that goal and became a professor at Platteville College (later became the University of Wisconsin at Platteville) and had a small farm with a small herds of cattle. *Even after retirement I still do not consider myself having attained my goal in life.*

We made a deal that whoever got back to the apartment first would cook. He usually cooked. I felt so bad about it that I came home earlier at least once a week to cook. He liked to bake cookies and bread. I learned from him but never was very good. One habit he got from me was to have green tea after dinner, usually mixed with toasted rice grains. He liked to shop and looked for bargains. He bought a hindquarter of beef from the university experimental farm. We cut it up, wrapped it in two servings per package, and kept the packages in a freezer rented at a market.

He had two bicycles, and I usually borrowed one. We rode to Picnic Point at the end of a peninsula of Lake Mendota often as exercise. We occasionally went to a pier off Lake Mendota and got clams; we did not worry about the possibility of the lake being polluted. We did not get sick from eating them nor were we aware of getting parasites from them.

Professor Cross had suggested that I do research with Dr. John Margrave, a high-temperature chemist, who was a promising young professor. I went to see him as soon as I got to the Chemistry Department. He suggested two or three projects. I chose a solar furnace project because it sounded like something new. I was probably influenced by the wartime Manchuria where fuel was scarce. The solar furnace was a large glass tube at the focal point of a military surplus searchlight. The objective was to synthesize carbon tetrachloride in the furnace by sticking a carbon rod inside the tube surrounded by chlorine gas and seal the ends by melting the ends of the glass tube. I stood by the searchlight all winter long to collect the products. I analyzed the products by mass spectroscopy after each experiment. There may have been carbon tetrachloride, but it was a minor product among many other chlorine compounds. I do not remember what I tried to make the reactions to favor carbon tetrachloride synthesis. The only advice I got from Dr. Margrave was that I should study the literature more. This was before the day of instant information through the Internet. I was looking at chemical abstracts with not much success. By the time spring came, I was completely depressed. The idea for the project probably occurred to Margrave because one of the methods in use around that time was to synthesize carbon tetrachloride from carbon disulfide and chlorine gas at a high temperature. Even to this day, I think no one has ever succeeded in making carbon tetrachloride by the process I was using. It is a highly toxic chemical, and subsequently, its use has been discouraged.

Around that time in the spring semester, I took a preliminary examination and got a high grade in physical chemistry but flunked analytical chemistry. I had another chance in the fall, but I lost interest.

One day at the University Book Store, I noticed a small book by *Scientific American* titled *The Physics and Chemistry of Life*, 1955. The book fascinated me. Dr. Robert Burris of the Biochemistry Department at the University of Wisconsin was mentioned as a pioneer in research on nitrogen fixation and photosynthesis. On the spur of the moment, I went to see Dr. Burris. He told me that with my strong background in physical chemistry, I should go into physical biochemistry instead of photosynthesis and nitrogen fixation. He immediately took me to Dr. Paul Kaesberg, a biophysicist and assistant professor working on physical chemical characterization of plant viruses. He hired me on the spot as a research assistant, and thus I became a physical biochemist. I was assigned to characterize a cucumber mosaic virus by an analytical ultracentrifuge.

Our laboratory was in the middle section of the third floor in the new addition to the Biochemistry Department. The floor was occupied by the laboratories of three assistant professors: Dr. Robert Baldwin, Dr. Paul Kaesberg, and Dr. Robert Bock. Among the three Dr. Bock impressed me the most; he appeared to know everything. He asked questions during seminars most frequently. *In retrospect he was the only one among the three who was not elected to the National Academy of Sciences.*

Soon after Bob Hansen got married, I moved in with two colleagues from the third floor laboratories. Our apartment was on Dayton Street. The boys were Hiroshi Yamazaki and Art Saponara. We also had a fourth roommate, Isao Hashimoto, from the Soil Department. The apartment was the third floor of a house owned by an old person in a wheelchair. He probably never went up to the third floor. The rent was sixty dollars per month or fifteen for each of us.

The previous tenant was an Indian family. They moved to the University of California-Berkeley. They left all the furniture, which we promised to pay for later. When we moved in, we were shocked. The sink was full of dirty dishes and pans; *more than fifty years later, I still use one of the cast-iron frying pans almost every morning.* When we opened a cabinet drawer, we found a mouse nest with baby mice. When we opened a closet, a bat flew out. We were so upset; we never paid for the furniture.

I think Hiroshi was the most serious student of the group. He generally went to bed first. Art went to bed last. He liked to do abstract oil painting late at night, and I usually watched him paint. I do not remember how Paul Kaesberg got a chance to see Art's painting because Art was not his student, but he did, and he liked the painting so much that he got it and hung it in his living room. Perhaps because of Art's influence, I like modern abstract paintings better than medieval European paintings. However, I like Japanese brush paintings with charcoal the best. They express nature best with just a few strokes.

Isao came from Japan but lived in Hawaii for a while and interacted with his Hawaiian friends. A bunch of them lived across the street from us. They were more friendly and outgoing than the Japanese Americans of the West Coast. We went to their annual luau and watched Hawaiian Japanese girls performing hula dances all day long. We ate their pig—a whole pig steam cooked in a laboratory autoclave. The pig was from nearby Oscar Meyer and was free. They got pineapples and poi free from Hawaii, courtesy of Pan Am. They impressed me with their skills of getting free food.

One day Isao took Hiroshi and me to the home of his friend Hara for a dinner. To my surprise I found out Mr. Hara was from Seattle and had worked as an accountant for my grandparents at their Detroit Hotel in the 1930s. I immediately wrote to mom about him, and she remembered him well.

Prior to the end of the war, the Japanese were permitted to move out of the relocation centers as long as they did not go back to the West Coast. Many relocated to other areas permanently. I met two other family friends of my grandparents in Chicago when I visited. One was Mrs. Fumi Nakamura, a cousin of my grandmother and father. Her husband was gone by the time I met her. She had three children; her two sons were living with her.

One was a chemical engineer, and his picture appeared in an issue of *American Chemical Engineering News* while I was a graduate student at Wisconsin. Another was an accountant who had interacted with my mother while they were kids in Seattle. Other family friends were Mr. and Mrs. Hori. *They used to send us boxes of Baby Ruth and Butterfinger while we lived in Opportunity, Washington. Mr. Hori probably worked at Nestle. Even now, those two chocolate bars are my favorites.*

The conversation I remembered most from the early period of graduate school with my biochemistry peers on the third floor was the genetic code. We concluded that it would not be solved within our lifetime. Yet the code was found to be a triplet non-overlapping code by the time I got my PhD degree in 1961. Dr. Paul Kaesberg came back from the International Congress of Biochemistry in Moscow where Marshall Nirenberg and Heinrich Matthaei of the National Institute of Health, Bethesda MD, reported that UUU triplet is the code for phenylalanine. *By 1966 the genetic codes for all natural amino acids were found. Another key contributor was Dr. Gobind Khorana of the Enzyme Institute at the University of Wisconsin. The Enzyme Institute hired him while I was a student. He became famous for developing the method of synthesis of oligonucleotides with defined sequences while he was at the University of British Columbia. All life forms on Planet Earth have the same code; the code is universal, consistent with the theory that all lives evolved from a common ancestor.*

I received my master of science degree in 1959 on the thesis titled: "The Identification of Cucumber Mosaic Virus isolated from Pumpkin Leaves." My goal was to isolate the virus and determine that it was an RNA-protein complex. I found that the virus was RNA covered with a protein coat. For this project I grew pumpkin plants on a field on the west side of the campus. I infected the pumpkin leaves with plant juice extracted from previously infected plant leaves using a mortar and pestle with carborundum as an abrasive. The virus was isolated from plant leaves, purified, and characterized mostly using a Spinco analytical ultracentrifuge, the most popular instrument used by biophysical chemists of that period. The infectious particle was a spherical nuclear protein particle with a molecular weight of about five million.

After getting my Master of Science degree, I started to date girls on my own initiative. My shyness was mostly gone, but I was not able to express my feelings to any of them. I interacted with girls on our floor at school—playing tennis, going to concerts and Rats Keller at the student union. One night soon after getting my MS, I was watching a Hawaiian Japanese girl performing a hula dance at the Rats Keller. She threw a flower at me, and we started to date, but I was more interested in her roommate. However, this roommate was more interested in a Vietnamese student, and I interacted with both girls together. I even sent only one valentine card to the two girls. We went to Hawaiian parties together, which lasted all night. I went home around midnight and came back the next morning to pick them up. One guy I remember was going to be a preacher. He sat quietly throughout the evening and watched us, without drinking.

I also dated a Japanese student from Tokyo, Ms. Fukuda; we mostly went to restaurants and talked in English. Some years later my cousin Hideko told me that she learned English from Fukuda san. Ms. Fukuda told Hideko that she knew me in Madison—a small world.

Another incident that made me feel that the world was small was a phone call I received from a Seattle boy stationed at the air force base in Madison. One day I came back to our apartment early and heard the phone ringing. I rushed up the stairs to our third floor unit and answered it. It was from a Japanese American boy at the air force base. He said he'd just come to Madison and did not know anyone. He looked up the city phone directory, started to search for a Japanese name, and came across my name. He said he was from Seattle, and I replied I was born there. He said he had a sister who was a Pan American Airline stewardess; I said my sister was also a Pan Am stewardess and stationed in Hawaii. As it turned out, my sister, Irene, and his sister were roommates. We also had brothers who were going to Garfield High School in Seattle. I invited him to our apartment and then introduced him to the Hawaiian boys living across the street from us. They were about the same age, but he did not stay very long in Madison. He requested a transfer and moved back to Seattle the first chance he got.

For my PhD thesis, Professor Kaesberg suggested I characterize the Phi-X 174 bacteriophage. Dr. Robert Sinsheimer found that this bacteriophage had a spherical shape and contained single-stranded DNA. Professor Kaesberg liked to work with the simplest viruses, and so it was natural for him to have an interest in it. Until I got involved with this bacteriophage, I had never worked with microorganisms and did not take a course in microbiology. Perhaps because of my inexperience, I had difficulties preparing large quantities of Phi-X 174. Electron microscopy had shown me that it is often contaminated by bacteriophage T1. Just about that time, the annual meetings of Federation of American Societies of Experimental Biology were held in Chicago. I went and sought Sinsheimer's advice. He told me as if it was common knowledge that I should have been using the host *E. coli* resistant to T1 phage. Then why didn't he send me that host when we requested the Phi-X 174 from him? I learned that bacteriophage T1 is ubiquitous and difficult to get rid of once it contaminated equipment. The greatest contamination occurred when a postdoctoral fellow of Dr. Khorana (who later won a Nobel Prize) inoculated *E. coli* with Phi-X 174 in the five-hundred-gallon tank at the fermentation laboratory. To his surprise it was mostly T1. He got so discouraged that he quit. I heard that for many years after that, that contaminated fermenter was not used.

Then in February of 1960, Dr. Kaesberg let Hiroshi Yamazaki and me attend a Biophysical Society meeting in Philadelphia. It was the first time I traveled on a commercial plane. Hiroshi had joined Kaesberg's laboratory almost the same time I did, in the summer of 1957. He already had a master's degree from Hokkaido

University in Japan and started to work on his PhD as soon as he came. We did not talk to each other in Japanese. At the Biophysical Society meetings, he presented a talk on wild cucumber mosaic virus, his PhD thesis project. I was not making any progress with my project.

On the afternoon of February 26, I heard a talk by W. Weidel on the receptors of bacteriophage T5. The T-phage (T5 is an example) invades its host bacterium by injecting its DNA through its tail while attached to its specific receptor on the bacterial surface. I was very much intrigued by his talk. I decided to work on the invasion of a spherical phage, Phi-X 174, to its host. I thought that the mechanism of invasion by a simple spherical phage would be much simpler to elucidate than T-phages. More importantly I did not have to prepare a large quantity of the phage. I wanted to go back to Madison immediately to propose the project to Kaesberg. However, Hiroshi and I had made the plan previously to go to New York to see the city and enjoy its culture.

While in Philadelphia we took a tour of the city and went to its museum where I was impressed to see a teahouse within the museum building and Independence Hall with its bell. I was in Japan immediately after the war and did not go anywhere; therefore, this was the first time I saw any of Japanese arts. It was the first time I saw the tea room properly set up for the tea ceremony. The Fujimuras lived briefly in the tearoom at our uncle's house (Chapter 6), but we never saw that room properly set up for tea ceremony.

Then we stayed in New York for three days. We took an all-day tour of Manhattan Island, went up the Empire State Building, and up the arm of the Statue of Liberty. At a theater on Broadway, we saw Flower Drum Song performed by Pat Suzuki. We went to a Japanese movie, Ikiru, at Little Carnegie and another show at Radio City Hall, which included stage shows and ended with can-can girls kicking their legs in unison. We went to the Metropolitan and Guggenheim Museums. I was impressed with the unique structure of the Guggenheim Museum, designed by Frank Lloyd Wright, and its modern art. I realized that I enjoy looking at modern abstract paintings more than old portraits. We went to a French restaurant for dinner one night but were not impressed. Another evening we went to Sukiyaki, one of the three Japanese restaurants on Manhattan Island. We ate sashimi, yakisoba, and some other dishes. *There were no sushi restaurants in New York then. It was unthinkable in those days that eventually there would be hundreds of sushi restaurants on Manhattan, and sushi would come to be known almost as well as hamburgers. I heard a saying that Harvard imported sushi, and Japan imported hamburger.* We think we saw in three days everything a tourist should see in Manhattan, and we were obviously biased toward Japanese culture.

My habit of going to church on Sunday continued in Madison without joining a church. I went to many different denominations including Unitarian, but I most frequently attended the Wesley Foundation of the Methodist Church nearby the campus. Whenever a preacher said something I was strongly against, I stopped going for a while but eventually resumed. I was perturbed when a preacher said or implied that Christians are better than non-Christians. I have both Christian and non-Christian friends, and I could not distinguish between the two based on their character, dependability, and compassion.

I got my PhD in August 1961 on the thesis titled "A Study of the Mechanism of Invasion by the Spherical Phage φX174." It was eventually published in the *Biophysical Journal* (1962) with the title "The Adsorption of Bacteriophage φX174 to Its Host" with Paul Kaesberg as the coauthor. It was the first publication on the subject, and Nino Incardona, a colleague at Kaesberg's laboratory, made it into his lifetime project. Detailed elucidation on mechanisms of adsorption and penetration was made much later by Arthur Kornberg's laboratory at Stanford (1975). (Arthur Kornberg received the Nobel Prize for his discovery of DNA polymerase.) Our paper was cited in their first paper on the subject. I felt honored to be cited by such an illustrious scientist. Another scientist I met at a meeting around that time told me that Salvador Luria, one of the original investigators in molecular biology and another Nobel Prize recipient, told him to cite our paper in his paper related to the subject. I was not aware that my PhD thesis was so well recognized.

Hiroshi Yamazaki got his PhD about a year before I received my PhD and went back to Japan to get married to a girl through his mother's connection. He came back and one day suggested that I should go to Japan as a postdoctoral fellow. I was not thinking along that line and asked Kaesberg for his opinion. He agreed; he thought Japan was doing important research in molecular biology and I should go. I applied to three places: Dr. Fujio Egami at Tokyo University, Dr. Itaru Watanabe at Kyoto University, and Dr. Masayasu Nomura at Osaka University. Drs. Egami and Watanabe were world famous. Dr. Nomura was a young molecular biologist who had just come back from doing outstanding research in the United States. Dr. Bunji Hagihara, who was a professor at the medical school of Osaka University and a visiting investigator at the Enzyme Institute where I met him at the early period of my graduate work, suggested Dr. Nomura to me.

All three had shown interest in having me, but Dr. Nomura's research projects were closest to my interest, and his laboratory had an excellent facility with sufficient support from the US National Institute of Health. I received a postdoctoral fellowship from the National Institute of Health for my financial support and travel expenses.

Prior to leaving for Japan, I found a place to stay. I had been exchanging letters with Sadakazu Hasegawa who had come back from Dalian, Manchuria, and lived in Osaka. I asked him to find me a place to stay. He found a place for me in Shukugawa, Nishinomiya, through Mrs. Tomi Ichikawa, his aunt. Nishinomiya is a residential suburb between Osaka and Kobe. Shukugawa is its subdivision along a river lined by pine and cherry trees; it is a beautiful site in springtime.

PART III:

A BIOCHEMIST IN
MOLECULAR BIOLOGY

CHAPTER 13:
POSTDOCTORAL YEAR AT OSAKA UNIVERSITY (DECEMBER, 1961– DECEMBER, 1962)

13-1: Uncle Yoshiwada's Family in Tokyo

Ironically, I went to Osaka University as a postdoctoral fellow in molecular biology, funded by the US National Institute of Health, at a time when the Japanese were coming to the United States as postdoctoral fellows to learn molecular biology.

My younger sister, Irene, was a stewardess for Pan American, and I flew on the same plane with her to the Tokyo Haneda Airport. At a stopover in Honolulu, Irene had arranged for me to have an all-night party and got a box of pineapples from her friend. The party was enjoyable with many pretty, young, and friendly girls. On the plane Irene had introduced me to a man whose nephew was a biochemist. He gave me his nephew's name, but I stuck it into my wallet without looking at it.

At the Haneda airport, The Yoshiwadas were at the balcony deck and shouted at me, "Kan-chan," as I got off the plane. I had not heard anyone call me by my Japanese name since fourteen years earlier when the Yoshiwadas and my father had sent us off from Yokohama harbor (chapter 7). As I went through customs at Haneda, I must have looked lost. I overheard an official talking about me with another, saying that I probably did not understand Japanese.

I gave the box of pineapples to Uncle and Aunt Yoshiwada and never had a chance to taste even a slice. Subsequently, I learned that it is a Japanese custom not to open a gift from a guest in his presence. They had a welcome party for me at Hideko's house. She had married a nephew of the owner of Prince Automobile Company (which subsequently had merged with Nissan) and lived in a beautiful semiwestern Japanese home. We had a gourmet dinner, which was a mixture of Western and Japanese dishes. Japanese Americans on the West Coast served similar combinations of dishes.

Uncle Yoshiwada took three of us, his son Tetsuo and his nephews Yukio Kamada, and me, to his favorite hangouts when I visited Tokyo. On Christmas holidays I stayed with the Yoshiwadas. We went out with Tetsuo as the driver, but he drank as much as the rest of us; *the regulation about drunk driving was not strict then.* We first went to Al-salon (abbreviation for albeit salon;

the Japanese do these kinds of combinations of foreign words and abbreviate them), which was a dance hall with many office girls working as hostesses in the evening. We had beers there but did not dance. Then we went to Uncle's favorite sushi bar for sake and something to eat. I still remember that I ate sushi with a dancing shrimp (this means the shrimp was still moving) on the top of a nigiri sushi. Then for the nightcap we went to his favorite bar where we had whiskey. The girls there seemed to know my uncle well. Uncle Yoshiwada introduced us three boys as his sons, each from different mothers. *In retrospect he was like the father of Yukio and me because Yukio lost his father a long time ago and stayed in Uncle's house in the past, and during my marriage ceremony (next chapter), Uncle Yoshiwada acted as my father.*

This way of going around drinking was common among Japanese working men and was called *hashigo*, a ladder. On New Year 's Day, a couple of these girls came to Uncle's house for the New Year's Day greeting. They brought boxes of hard candies. Aunt Yoshiwada greeted them without showing any sign of perturbation; apparently, it is a routine affair at the beginning of each year. However, she gave me that box of candies almost immediately afterward.

Around the time of my arrival in Japan, when we went into a bar, I asked a girl where I am from. She answered I probably came from Hawaii or Okinawa. A few months later, I asked the same question to another bar girl, and I was told I must be from somewhere between Tokyo and Osaka. I was satisfied to learn that my Japanese had improved so much that they could no longer tell I was a *gaijin* (foreigner).

13-2: Nomura's Laboratory at the Institute for Protein Research

I went to work for Dr. Masayasu Nomura at Institute for Protein Research, which is affiliated with the Osaka University School of Medicine in Nakanoshima, an island south of the Osaka railroad station. He was just starting as a *Jokyouju*, which is equivalent to an associate professor in American universities. The director of the institute was Professor Akabori, a world famous organic chemist. Soon after I came, he became the president of Osaka University.

All of us commuted to work on electric trains or streetcars. I commuted from Kurakuenguchi to Osaka Central Station by Hankyu, which is one of the major commuter train systems linking Kobe, Osaka, and Kyoto. The first time I tried to go to the Institute for Protein Research, I called Dr. Nomura to ask how to get there from the Osaka railroad station. I said I was standing near Senmon Daiten, but I was not sure that I was reading the Chinese characters correctly. He replied that he did not know such a store. Therefore, I took a taxi; the driver took me across the river from Nakanoshima at the front of the Microbiology Department. The driver did not know where the Institute for Protein Research was. I got off the taxi and asked a person walking by where it was. Following the direction I arrived at the Institute and got to Nomura's laboratory. Later, I learned there was a store named Senmon Daiten at the station; Nomura was from Tokyo and did not know much about the area, even inside the railroad station. I received an unlimited pass for commuter trains for free, rode the train to the station, and then walked about fifteen minutes to the laboratory. I could use the pass an unlimited number of times every day of the week.

We worked hard from morning to night but quit in time to catch the last train around midnight. Dr. Koji Okamoto, Nomura's *joshu*, was the busiest (a joshu is equivalent to an assistant professor but generally does not have an independent project); he often missed the last train and caught a taxi to go home. On a low salary, it must have been hard for him to do so. Besides Dr. Okamoto, Dr. Nomura had two visiting scientists, Dr. Kenichi Matsubara and Dr. Keiichi Hosokawa. In addition he had a graduate and an undergraduate student, two girls as technicians, and a secretary.

The laboratory was well equipped with American instruments, better than the third floor Biochemistry Department at the University of Wisconsin. Nomura's laboratory was in Kurahashi's section separated by a little space where we often had tea. Professor Kiyoshi Kurahashi came back from the US National Institutes of Health (NIH) where he was already well established. Both laboratories were well funded by the NIH. Dr. Kurahashi had two joshus, Drs. Toshio Fukasawa and Hiroshi Nikaido. Dr. Nikaido left the laboratory soon after I got there and went to the University of California at Berkeley; *he became a tenured professor and stayed there the rest of his career*. Drs. Kurahashi and Nomura had completely independent projects and did not interact much scientifically. I did talk about my PhD thesis to Kurahashi's section.

One night soon after my arrival, I told Matsubara that I met a person from Kanazawa on the plane whose nephew is a biochemist. I took out the piece of paper thinking to ask him if he knew the person, and I read the name, Kenichi Matsubara. Both of us were surprised. Among my peers in Japan, he was unusually self-confident and spoke with professors freely. *He became a well-known scientist in molecular biology.*

13-3: Research Projects at Nomura's Laboratory

Dr. Nomura micromanaged his group's projects; he gave in detail what each of us was going to do prior to each experiment. I joined the project on the effect of the bacteriophage T4 infection on its host functions. My role was to analyze the physical integrity of phage DNA in its host bacteria. By summer we had shown that there was no extensive degradation of the host DNA, but the function of the host DNA ceased almost instantly after the phage infection. The findings were published that year in the *Journal of Molecular Biology* (Nomura, et al., 1962), a prestigious journal in the field that came into existence in 1959, the year I started on my PhD thesis project.

The manuscript based on my PhD thesis was published in the same year in *Biophysical Journal* (Fujimura and Kaesberg, 1962), which came into existence the year

I got my PhD, 1961. Without being aware, I got into a very competitive field where new, exciting discoveries were published frequently. Proceedings of the National Academy of Sciences that publishes significant new discoveries in all sciences was dominated by the findings in molecular biology for many decades.

During the summer Nomura went to Mathew Meselson's laboratory at Harvard University. Dr. Meselson is well-known for developing an elegant technique of cesium chloride (CsCl) equilibrium density gradient centrifugation, which separated newly synthesized DNA labeled with a denser precursor than the preexisting DNA. The result showed that DNA replicates by a semiconservative mechanism, which means that double stranded DNA replicates by copying each strand with the newly incorporated precursors.

While Nomura was gone, I studied possible mechanisms for the synthesis of messenger RNA in a bacteriophage system thinking I would do research on it for the remaining period of my stay. For this I read work by Dr. Elliot Volkin, at Oak Ridge National Laboratory, who discovered a type of RNA with the sequence similar to that of the infecting phage DNA, which came to be known as messenger RNA. *I did not dream that about a year from then, I would be hired by Dr. Volkin.* Messenger RNA transcribes messages coded in DNA to be translated into proteins on the surface of ribosomes, which are made up of two nuclear protein particles each of which consists of RNA coated with proteins. Their structure and function were not known in detail at that time.

When Dr. Nomura came back, he appeared disinterested in what I did during the summer. Instead he asked me to physical chemically characterize ribosomal particles remaining after CsCl density gradient centrifugation to equilibrium. During the centrifugation ribosome was stripped of much of its coat proteins by a high concentration of CsCl and became smaller and formed in a centrifuge tube a single denser band than the original ribosome. What I noticed was that after the centrifugation a huge amount of proteins had floated to the top of the solution in the centrifuge tube, and the remaining particles banded in the tube at the position in the CsCl solution equal in density to the particles. My project was to collect these particles, which were called CsCl particles; dialyze out CsCl; and determine their size.

One day out of curiosity I collected the protein fraction that floated to the top of the CsCl solution during centrifugation, dialyzed out CsCl, and recombined it with the CsCl particles. I found out, to my surprise, the ribosomal particles of the original size were recovered. Nomura realized the significance of the result. This suggested that complete ribosomal particles could be reconstituted from ribosomal RNA and proteins. He asked me not to work on this project after I leave his laboratory and not to talk to anyone about this finding. He wanted to work on the reconstitution of ribosomes in his own laboratory. I left the laboratory soon afterward and did not pursue the finding any further.

Subsequently, he had moved to the University of Wisconsin and succeeded in the reconstitution of the functional ribosome by fractionating the protein fraction and adding back the proteins in the proper sequence to the purified RNA (circa 1963–1973). This accomplishment made him world famous, and he was elected to the National Academy of Sciences. Subsequently, several times I heard rumors that he had been nominated as a candidate for the Nobel Prize. When the researchers on ribosome structures won the Nobel Prize in Chemistry for 2009, I would have expected Nomura to be included, but he was not.

13-4: Social Activities with the Laboratory Members

We were very friendly to each other in the laboratory and occasionally went on picnics and sight-seeing trips to surrounding areas. When we went to a shrine or temple, the explanations of the site were usually written on a couple of wooden boards positioned side by side, one in Old Japanese the other in English. I teased the young technicians by asking them what these notices said—they could not read the Old Japanese. I explained to them what these notes said, translating from English; they were amazed at how well I knew.

One day a visiting scientist, Dr. M. Nakamura, asked would I want to go to a geisha house. I said sure; it probably would be the first and the last time I would have a chance to go. He also asked Drs. Okamoto and Nomura. We went to one in Gion, Kyoto, the most famous geisha district. I learned that a geisha is a lady who plays a musical instrument, while a *maiko* performs traditional dance clad in a bright colored kimono; Maiko is around twenty years old. The image of a geisha I had, and Americans have in general, actually is a maiko. We enjoyed watching a *mai* performed by a maiko following the music played by a geisha. The mai is a traditional dance performed in a front of a small number of guests in a private room of a geisha house. It is quite different from a *buyou*, which is a traditional dance performed on a stage in front of an audience in a theater. The style of dancing appears the same to a nonobservant person like me. Early evenings in the Gion district, maikos often walked around clad in bright kimonos.

CHAPTER 14:
MARRIAGE WITH SHIGEKO

The Ichikawas had two daughters. The older, Noriko, was married and had just had a baby son, and the younger one, Shigeko, was two years younger than I, the same age as my sister, June. I was introduced to her the first day I visited their house.

The place I was staying, the Kojimas, was within walking distance from the Ichikawas. The Kojimas had a son, Yoshikazu, and his wife, Hisako, living with them. Hisako was a friend of Noriko, and through their relationship I was introduced to live in the Kojimas house. It was a semi-Western style house with a beautiful garden. The reason I accepted the room was because it had a Western style toilet, which was not very common then; I had a problem with squatting over a Japanese style toilet. I got a room with a bunk bed and a desk, and Mrs. Ichikawa bought me a mattress for the bed. Sadakazu got me a space heater to warm up the room. Mrs. Kojima served me breakfast every morning. She also cleaned my room, which I was not aware of until Shigeko told me after I left the place.

Shigeko acted frequently as my guide and took me around Kyoto, Nara, and Osaka. We went to most of the famous places and many special events. We went to the Gion Festival, an annual event famous for its parade consisting of *mikoshi*, a uniquely designed portable shrine. Its small models are sold everywhere around the district. It is also the time maikos of the prestigious district perform on a stage. These maikos also demonstrate tea ceremonies. We went there a few days after my colleagues and I went to the geisha house. We went into a tea ceremony, and I was surprised that the lady performing the ceremony was the same maiko who had performed for my colleagues and me. I waived at her spontaneously, and Shigeko got upset. She said it is improper to wave at someone performing on a stage.

The Ichikawa family was devout Methodist. I went with them to their church frequently. Shigeko's mother was a daughter of a samurai and brought up Shigeko as a proper daughter of a samurai. I treated Shigeko as a distant relative not a girlfriend.

One summer day Kimi Sakuyama, the eldest daughter of the Hasegawa, called me on the phone and said Shigeko would like to marry me. I was quite surprised. I did not think a girl like Shigeko would marry me and go far away from her home. Her mother was a very caring person, and the Ichikawa family lived surrounded by close friends and relatives, mostly Christians. I replied I would talk directly with Shigeko, thinking she would not want to lead the kind of life I had in the States.

My siblings and I did not have an enjoyable, stable family as we grew up. We moved from America to Manchuria to Japan and back to America. We did not have

much of a family life. Our father was absent most of our childhood when we needed him the most. Back in the States, our mother had divorced him and worked at the Ritz Café during the daytime while we lived in Opportunity. After graduating from Central Valley High School, I moved to Seattle and then to Madison and did not know where I would settle down. Madison

Photo 14: Shigeko, my bride

is far away from my family, and I had not interacted with them much. When I visited them occasionally, my brother and sisters' friends were surprised that June was not the eldest among the siblings. I did not think Shigeko would get married to a person with my background. However, I felt she was the ideal girl for me to establish a stable family life.

One evening soon afterward, Shigeko and I went to Kobe Harbor and talked at a pier. In essence I said the life in the States is difficult, and I have only a few close friends, and she may feel lonely, but she accepted to marry me. I was surprised and wrote to my mother that I was getting married to a girl who is like a Buddha in looks and character (Photo 14).

I learned a few years after our marriage that without my knowledge, Kimi and Sadayo, her sister, suggested me to the Ichikawas as the groom for Shigeko. They agreed, and Shigeko obeyed her parents. In a traditional Japanese family, parents decide whom their children get married to. Uncle Setsuzo Kawamura and his wife were devout Christians, and the Ichikawas apparently assumed I was like my uncle. My uncle had graduated at the top of his class in chemistry at Tokyo University, and here I came with a PhD degree in biochemistry from Wisconsin to do research at one of the top universities in Japan. They decided I'd grown up in a proper family. I am also indebted to Sadakazu for introducing me to the Ichikawa family, although he did not have any intention of me getting married to his favorite cousin and taking her far away. Mrs. Tomi Ichikawa and my Uncle Setsuzo Kawamura's wife, Teru, were sisters. Mrs. Hasegawa, whom I met in Dalian, was also their sister. (Mrs. Hasegawa died from uterine cancer during the war.) I learned much later from Shigeko that Mrs. Ichikawa and my father were at the wedding of Uncle Setsuzo while my father was still a college student in Osaka (1920s). Therefore, both Shigeko and I are cousins of Uncle Setsuzo's children. In one of her visits to Uncle Setsuzo's place, Shigeko met my father, who was staying there in the early 50s. Therefore, Shigeko was familiar with my father. Apparently, I was the only one who did not know these relationships.

My assignment at Nomura's laboratory was finished at the end of November, so Shigeko and I got married on December 1 at Osaka Christian Center with Reverend Seno of the Ichikawa's church officiating. Shigeru Sakuyama was an official intermediary. *Shigeru was Kimi's husband and an engineer who worked for the Russians in Dalian for several years after the war. After coming back to Japan, he became the director of research and a member of the board of directors of Nippon Shokubai, a chemical company specialized in catalysts technology.*

The surprise guests were two of my former middle school classmates from Hofu, Yamaguchi. I took them to a lunch at a restaurant that specialized in shabushabu in which vegetables were cooked in a wok in front of us, and each of us was provided with thin slices of beef that we cooked one slice at a time by dipping them in the wok for a few seconds. We had a leisurely feast. We got to the wedding just fifteen minutes prior to the ceremony. I thought we had left the restaurant with ample time, but the taxi driver took us to the wrong place, and I had to redirect him. We were going to practice the ceremony, but there was no time for that. Shigeko said everyone was worried, *and in retrospect she wished that I had never shown up.*

We had the reception immediately following the ceremony. Shigeru and Kimi Sakuyama shared the table with us, and Shigeru toasted for us. Uncle Motosuke Yoshiwada from Tokyo was my father substitute. Uncle Yoshiwada said in his speech that I came to Japan for *yuugaku*, which means to learn to play around; he certainly taught me how to drink around Tokyo, moving from one bar to another. Everyone from the laboratories of Nomura and Kurahashi was there. Grandmother's sister, Kikuko, and the wife of her stepbrother, Takao, were also present. Shigeko looked happy going around to her friends. We were so busy interacting with the guests that we forgot to eat our wedding cake. I also forgot to thank the Ichikawas for giving me their daughter.

For our honeymoon we went to Washuzan, a small village in the Okayama Prefecture by the Seto Inland Sea. Mrs. Ichikawa had arranged for us to stay at an inn by the sea. I still remember the taste of the dinner. It was gills of red snappers cooked in some kind of sauce based on soy sauce (aradaki). It was delicious; *occasionally we reminisce about that trip over the dinner of aradaki prepared by Shigeko*. After a few days' stay with Shigeko's family, we went to Tokyo, stayed in an inn near Roppongi, and met our relatives and friends living in that area. Then we went to Nikko, a popular tourist site, for a couple of days and stayed at a hotel by Chuuzenji Lake and then left Japan.

CHAPTER 15:
SIGNIFICANCE OF MY POSTDOCTORAL PERIOD

15-1: Postdoctoral Period in Japan

The thirteen-month stay in Japan was highly significant. It made me a whole person. I could now converse freely in both Japanese and English. However, when I talked science to the Japanese, I needed to use English vocabulary, and I still have an accent in my English. I never tried to correct it. I was very shy and learned to pronounce many words by self-study.

Many years later I got two hypotheses for my improper accent. In 1996 Time *selected David Ho as the Man of the Year for his contribution in AIDS research. He spoke English without a Chinese accent. He credited his father for telling him not to learn English from a Chinese. He learned English after coming to America. I realized then that the reason for my accent was the Japanese English teachers I had in Manchuria and Hofu. My colleague at FDA (circa 1993) Dr. Marilyn Lightfoot gave me another possibility. She said I was tone deaf; such a person has problems learning to speak with a proper accent. I am a very poor singer. I still remember a test given in a first grade music class in Shenyang. I was to identify notes plucked on a piano keyboard. I got absolute zero.*

I made efforts to study Japanese history and culture; I am expected to be an expert on Japan by the Americans and an expert on America by the Japanese. The first book I purchased as soon as I got to Japan was a Japanese history book (M. Takayanagi and M. Watanabe, 1958) in which the dates were cited in Christian years, which attracted me to buy it.

The *Japanese count the years by the reign of each emperor; each reign starts as year one. The current era, Heisei, is the 125th emperor, which started in 1989, the year Emperor Showa died, which was Showa 64; it also was Heisei 1. I do not know anyone who could arrange the imperial years completely in the correct sequence. Until the end of the war, they calculated the number of years from the mystical beginning of the imperial reign, but that method of counting was abolished probably by a decree from the General Headquarters (GHQ) of General MacArthur. However, they still count the year by making the beginning of the reigning emperor as year one. The last year of the previous emperor and the first year of the new one is the same year, which makes the conversion very difficult. I do not know a mathematical formula that would do this.*

During the war Japanese history was taught beginning from the myth that a god created Japan. A god stirred the sea with a spear, and the drops from the spear became Japan's islands. Emperor Jimmu, the direct descendant of the sun goddess, established Japan in 660 BC. Japan had an elaborate ceremony in 1940 as the twenty-six hundredth year after the country was established. I was curious to see how they taught the origin of Japan now that it would be too ridiculous to teach the history beginning on a myth.

The history book by Takayanagi and Watanabe starts with geological evidence that Japan proper was located at the eastern edge of the Asia continent and went through several periods of rise and fall, connected to the continent or becoming islands, and finally became the present day islands. The oldest history book, *Nippon Shoki*, was written in 720AD, and there is no evidence Emperor Jimmu ever existed. The postwar history book states that Emperor Suijin, who died in 258AD, may have been the real first emperor (tenth in *Nippon Shoki*). This is not definite either, but the meaning of Suijin is similar to Jimmu, and there are archaeological remains of emperors starting in the third century. All emperors are direct descendants of Jimmu.

Scientifically, my greatest accomplishment as a postdoctoral fellow was to find that ribosomes could be reconstituted by adding to their RNAs with respective proteins in proper order. This became the major lifelong project of Professor Nomura. Nomura and his group members had convinced me that I should carry on basic research at some research institution instead of doing mission-oriented research at a private company laboratory. I was too shy to consider a professorship at a university.

However, the marriage to Shigeko turned out to be the greatest and luckiest event of my life as revealed in the rest of my memoir. I got her through the one and only Manchurian connection I kept up.

15-2: The Trip Back to the States with My Bride

We had more than a month for our honeymoon as we traveled slowly back to Madison via Hawaii, Seattle, and Spokane. We flew over the Pacific to Hawaii where we borrowed a car from my friend at the University of Hawaii, whom I befriended while he was at the University of Wisconsin. We tried to explore all around Oahu Island, but it was raining, so we just went to a nearby waterfall. Then we flew into San Francisco. We were indebted to Shigeko's family friend for taking us around San Francisco.

I made time to see two professors at Stanford University. I knew one of the professors, Robert Baldwin, who had his laboratory in the same room as I had at the University of Wisconsin. He had moved to Stanford University in 1959 when Arthur Kornberg had organized the Department of Biochemistry. He was a well-known authority on protein structure. Another was Dale Kaiser, who was famous for research in bacteriophage lambda. Both professors probably judged what I did in Japan were nothing new and exciting. As I had promised Nomura, I did not mention to them my most exciting finding about the reconstitution of ribosome.

We then went to Seattle to introduce my bride to my mother and my siblings. We spent Christmas there. The only thing I remember is that we went to a seafood restaurant by the Seattle harbor. Shigeko did not express her wish to go somewhere else. *About ten years later, she complained that I had not taken her to any Japanese restaurants during that stay in Seattle. I thought since we had just come from Japan it was unnecessary to go to any Japanese restaurants, besides, there were no sushi restaurants in Seattle in those days.*

We went to Spokane to introduce Shigeko to my grandmother and father. Grandmother took us to a sukiyaki restaurant, the only Japanese restaurant in town. They did not let us stay in their Great Northern Hotel but got us a room in a motel in a better section of the city.

15-3: A Short Stay in Madison: the Birth of Our First Child

We arrived in Madison around mid-January and bought a Rambler on the advice by Hiroshi. We stayed in a motel between Middleton and Madison for a few days. The temperature got down to minus-thirty degrees or lower. I carried the car battery inside to keep it warm, and the acid from the battery ate through my overcoat and gloves. It would have been cheaper to buy a new battery. We moved into a relatively new apartment. We had a Japanese war bride next door to us. She did not have any idea where she was. She told me she was somewhere deep inside California!

We met some Japanese families through Hiroshi and Toshiko. They became lifelong friends. *Shigeko tends to keep up friendship for a long time; now, we write about two hundred Christmas greetings every season. It is a major undertaking. I write the major part of our messages in both languages, and then Shigeko revises and adds personal notes to the Japanese messages.*

Our first child, Dan Paul, was born August 11, 1963, about three weeks earlier than expected and was born prior to the arrival of our doctor to the hospital. *As it turned out, none of our three children's' doctors accompanied their births.*

I made a rule that the first names of our babies were to be Japanese names that are easy to pronounce in English. Dan is a Japanese name even though it could be an English name; I asked my father to give the name an appropriate Chinese character. The character given for Dan, 断, means decisive. Paul is from my mentor Paul Kaesberg. I made only a short visit each day to the hospital to see Shigeko and our son. *She still complains about that. She became a friend of her roommate; they exchanged Christmas cards for a long time.*

15-4: My Research Project at Kaesberg's Laboratory

When I got back to the laboratory, Kaesberg's main interest was on an RNA bacteriophage, R17. Prior to the discovery of RNA phage, all bacteriophages were known to have DNA. RNA phage was simpler than φX174 that

I had worked on for my PhD thesis. I treated the RNA extensively with RNase, an enzyme that specifically digested RNA to short oligonucleotides fractionated by chromatography, and determined its molecular weight by summing up the fragments. The molecular weight was the same as determined by a conventional method. However, my main interest was in looking for a permanent job. Therefore, NK Shinha, an associate in the laboratory, took over the project and eventually published in *J Molecular Biology* (1965).

Through Dr. Kaesberg's grapevine, I found out that Dr. Elliot (Ken) Volkin had a position open at Oak Ridge National Laboratory in Tennessee, so I went for an interview. I felt Oak Ridge was an ideal place for me. I was looking for a small town where I could pursue research based on my curiosity, and Ken Volkin told me I could take up any projects I wanted. He was no longer working on DNA-like RNA, the finding that made him world famous. I accepted the offer and canceled another job interview I had at Los Alamos. We delayed our departure because of Dan's birth and arrived in Oak Ridge near the end of October. This was before interstate highways, and I was shocked that local people drove along curvy, mountainous roads at full speed even though they could not see ahead.

I had saved some money prior to the marriage, but by the time we got to Oak Ridge, the savings were gone. We had to borrow money from a bank to buy furniture and other necessities.

CHAPTER 16:
SENIOR STAFF, BIOLOGY DIVISION, OAK RIDGE NATIONAL LABORATORY (ORNL)

16-1: My Research Projects

I was able to do curiosity-driven research from the beginning—recently known as fishing. If I had to depend on a grant, I needed to work on hypothesis-driven research. Therefore, this kind of research was permissible only with a group that was motivated in finding a new concept, in a place like Oak Ridge National Laboratory, where we did not have to depend on an external source for funding the research.

Elliot (Ken) Volkin led the group. He was famous for discovering unstable RNA synthesized soon after bacteriophage T2 infection that has nucleotide composition similar to that of T2 DNA (Volkin E & Astrachan L, 1956). Their initial finding was repeated many times in his laboratory (1956–1962). It was confirmed by many other laboratories including Masayasu Nomura's while he worked with Sol Spigelman and Ben Hall. Volkin was invited to give talks at famous symposia such as The Chemical Basis of Heredity (1957), but he and Lazarus Astrachan were not credited as the discoverers of messenger RNA. A few years later (1961), François Jacob and Jacques Monod coined the word "messenger RNA" (RNA with DNA-like sequence) and proposed the existence of unstable RNA that transmits the coded message in DNA sequence to synthesize a specific protein. They were awarded the Nobel Prize in 1965 for their hypothesis. Sidney Brenner, François Jacob, and Mathew Meselson (1961) were credited as the investigators that confirmed the hypothesis. By the time I joined Volkin's laboratory in late 1963, Ken was no longer working on messenger RNA, and Astrachan had moved to another institution. I was disappointed, but he gave me the freedom to do anything I wanted. *Paul Berg, winner of the 1980 Nobel Prize in Chemistry, called the finding of Volkin and Astrachan an "unsung but momentous discovery of a fundamental mechanism in genetic chemistry" and a "seminal discovery that has never received its proper due." I am sure all those who were credited as discoverers of messenger RNA had read the papers by Volkin and Astrachan, and most, if not all, of them have heard Volkin presenting his finding. Jacob was one of the speakers at the symposium on Chemical Basis of*

Heredity (1957), and I am certain Jacob and Monod came up with their hypothesis on messenger RNA after their interaction with Volkin.

For bacteria and viruses including bacteriophages, most of their DNA consists of codes for genes, but for higher organisms only a small fraction of DNA sequence codes for genes. Initially, noncoding DNAs were called "junk DNA," but subsequently many of these sequences were found to transcribe RNAs that are involved in regulation of gene expression; these are still under intense studies. *Probably all the DNA sequences have some essential functions; many are not yet known (2012).*

When I joined the senior staff on Volkin's group, there were three other senior staff members each doing independent research and a postdoctoral fellow sharing the same office. We often stayed until midnight doing experiments and then went out for beers prior to going home. Our office was also the coffee room. It was a noisy place to study; I was doing experiments without thinking much—just trying to find something new. I did most of my thinking by the laboratory bench while waiting for the experimental results.

During coffee breaks we discussed many political and social issues. One that I specifically remember is a proposal by Charlie Mead that we should borrow as much money as possible. The more wealth one has the more money one can borrow. This was in the early 60s. Apparently, many Americans followed this philosophy and got into heavy debt. Heavy-spending consumers and investors caused the recession that started in 2008. As of this writing in 2012, about 9 percent of workers are unemployed.

Charlie Mead thought the most important process for life to exist and evolve is DNA recombination. He searched for the enzyme essential for such a process and found the DNA joining enzyme (DNA ligase). He presented his finding at the Federation of American Societies for Experimental Biology, the largest meetings for biological scientists, and published in the *Proceedings of the National Academy of Sciences* (1964), which is known to publish very significant new findings. *The first edition of the* Principles of Biochemistry *by Albert Lehninger, 1982, a classic, credited Charlie Mead as the discoverer of DNA ligase.*

However, Charlie liked to work by himself at his own pace and did not like to be the central figure in the field. Therefore, he built his house by Watts Bar Lake, the largest Tennessee Valley Authority (TVA) lake, and quit doing research and moved there. Initially, he sold and installed huge satellite TV antennae for houses around the lake and eventually settled down to make woodcrafts. I consider him my model for living—doing what one likes to do at one's own pace.

I was working on characterization of the structure of RNA of an RNA phage in Kaesberg's laboratory, and one of the interests of Nomura's laboratory was colicine E2, an agent that kills bacteria by inhibiting DNA, RNA, and protein synthesis. However, bacteriophage T4 synthesis proceeds in E2 treated cells. At Volkin's laboratory I integrated two projects, and this led to my first publication from the Biology Division, which was published in the *Journal of Molecular Biology* (1966). RNA bacteriophage has its own RNA replicating enzyme. Therefore, others had proposed that colicine would not affect RNA phage synthesis. My paper reported that viral RNA synthesis is inhibited by colicine E2. *Subsequently, others have reported that a subunit of the RNA replicating enzyme is a subunit of ribosome (1970).* I had data in the paper that ribosome synthesis is inhibited. Therefore, this is the likely mechanism of inhibition of phage RNA synthesis, but I did not mention it and did not continue on the project.

I was interested in doing projects at a periphery of major activity in molecular biology so that I would not be under the pressure of competitors but be able to keep up with the major developments in the field. Dr. Volkin suggested I study bacteriophage T5 because it was the least studied among bacteriophages. I did not realize at that time that the projects using this bacteriophage would become my major research project during my stay at the Biology Division.

The first project I had with bacteriophage T5 was characterization of DNA recombination/repair using a mutant inhibited for DNA replication at the high temperature in infected cells (1968–1974). Even at the nonpermissive temperature, there was a residual DNA synthesis. By genetic studies John Cairns had shown that there was more than one DNA polymerase in *E. coli* (1969). DNA in a cell is constantly corrected for incorporation of wrong nucleotides or for environmental damages such as radiation. This suggested to me the possibility that DNA repair and replication enzymes may be different, both coded by infecting phage.

I with my assistant, Barbara Roop, purified T5 DNA polymerase to homogeneity and found that there is only one polymerase coded by T5 (1976). *Many years later Arthur Kornberg wrote that "Purifying an enzyme is rewarding all the way, from first starting to free it from the mob of proteins in a broken cell to having it finally in splendid isolation" (For the Love of Enzymes, 1989).* It has been my most rewarding project. Most of the scientists of my generation or younger who had isolated an enzyme had an experienced mentor. Barbara and I did it by ourselves without having any mentor on the procedure. We decided to perform extensive characterization of the enzyme.

Just then, a graduate student joined me, expressing interest in working for his PhD using this T5 DNA polymerase (Das, 1975–1979). Most of our work on T5 DNA polymerase was done with the assistance of Ms. Barbara Roop, who worked for me for fourteen years.

We found that T5 DNA polymerase is capable of unwinding double stranded DNA, and like other DNA polymerases that are involved in replication, it is associated with 3′ to 5′ exonuclease. The template was copied faithfully in part because of the 3′ to 5′ exonuclease associated with the polymerase that removed wrong nucleotides added by mistakes. In the temperature-sensitive mutant, the catalytic site of the polymerase is inactive at the high temperature (43°C), but the function is reversibly activated when the temperature is lowered to 25°C. However, the exonuclease remained active at the high temperature.

Shishir Das found that T5 DNA polymerase is processive; that is, one enzyme elongates DNA primer at its 3' end by adding nucleotides one at a time complementary to the template instead of distributive, which means it comes off the primer-template after the addition of each nucleotide. When compared with several other DNA polymerases known at that time, we found it was the most processive DNA polymerase (Das and Fujimura, 1979). Das received his PhD characterizing this processivity (1979, thesis title: "The Proofreading Function of Bacteriophage T5-Induced DNA Polymerase"). He may not have been aware of it, but he was fortunate to study an enzyme not available anywhere else without ever being involved in its purification.

Probably, our study had induced others to characterize processivity of DNA elongation as one of the basic properties of DNA polymerases. Now a replicative DNA polymerase, in complex with other proteins (DNA replication complex), is known to elongate a primer by processively adding thousands of nucleotide along a template strand (DNA replication). Elucidation of this mechanism was made by studies in vitro using purified DNA polymerases and adding back their accessory proteins. This was carried out at many laboratories using different systems—reconstitution of DNA replication complex.

16-2: Symposium on DNA Replication, Repair, and Transcription

In 1979 I was selected to chair the organizing committee and the conference for the 1980 Biology Division Symposium in Gatlinburg, Tennessee. The symposium was held annually in Gatlinburg; the city is located at the major entrance to the Smoky Mountains National Park and is a popular destination for tourists, full of motels and restaurants. Every year it was a big event for the Biology Division; we invited several prominent scientists including some from other countries. For the 1980 symposium, we selected the theme "DNA-Multiprotein Interactions in Transcription, Replication, and Repair."

Many polymerases and accessory proteins are involved in these processes. We invited twenty-two scientists who were making significant contributions for these three processes essential for the existence of life. We obtained a grant from the National Science Foundation to provide support for the speakers from foreign countries—one for each major topic. These were Dr. Yukinori Hirota, National Institute of Genetics, Mishima, Japan, on the initiation site on DNA for DNA replication in *E. coli*; Dr. Moshe Yaniv, Pasteur Institute, Paris, France, on the expression of viruses in cancer cells; and Dr. John Cairns, Imperial Cancer Research Fund, London, England, on induced repair of DNA damaged by an alkylating agent, a common mutagen.

The symposium was held from March 24 to 27 and was highly successful and informative with several posters from other attendees. The conference was timely in pointing out the trend in research on DNA replication, transcription, and repair involving multiprotein complexes. The proceeding of the symposium was edited by Waldo Cohn and published in *Progress in Nucleic Acid Research and Molecular Biology,* volume 26, 1981.

In my field of DNA replication, the talk by Dr. Antero So, University of Miami, on DNA polymerase delta from calf thymus, which his laboratory had discovered, had the greatest impact. It has exonuclease for proof reading function to maintain fidelity of replication. Prior to that, for twenty years DNA polymerase alpha was thought to be the only polymerase involved in DNA replication in eukaryotes, but it did not have the proof reading exonuclease activity. Fred Bollum, formerly at the Biology Division, ORNL, had discovered it in calf thymus (published in 1960).

Eukaryotic DNA polymerases were named using the Greek alphabet in the chronological order of discovery (Burgers et al. 2001). Prior to the discovery of DNA polymerase delta, DNA polymerase beta was found to be involved in repair of DNA, and DNA polymerase gamma was found to replicate mitochondria DNA. Subsequent to the discovery of DNA polymerase delta, another eukaryotic DNA polymerase was found associated with exonuclease and named epsilon. Further studies by others have shown that DNA polymerase epsilon is involved in elongation of the leading strand of double helix, and DNA polymerase delta is involved in elongation of the lagging strand. The elongation mechanisms of the two stands are different; once initiated the leading strand is continuously elongated, and the lagging strand is elongated in a stretch of short strands at the replication fork.

Reiji Okazaki proposed this mechanism for the lagging strand synthesis in 1968 based on his experiments and these short strands are called Okazaki fragments. He died of leukemia soon afterward due to the radiation exposure at Hiroshima; he was exposed looking for his parents soon after the atomic bomb explosion.

Subsequent studies have shown that DNA polymerase alpha-primase complex is involved in the initiation of DNA replication; RNA primer is required for the initiation of DNA replication. Primase initially synthesize a short RNA oligonucleotide, which is elongated for a short stretch by DNA polymerase alpha. Then DNA polymerase delta and epsilon take over for extensive elongation. All of these polymerases are in complex with other proteins to increase efficiency of elongation (processivity) and accuracy of copying the template strand (fidelity).

Recently, more DNA polymerases were found in eukaryote. These are involved in replication across damage in double helical structures and are known as translesion DNA polymerases. Mechanisms of DNA replication in eukaryote is complex, involving different polymerases specific for different DNA structures and functions. As suggested by the Greek alphabet, as of this writing, thirteen DNA polymerases are known.

The other two processes involving DNA transcription and repair also involve protein complexes, and their mechanisms are even more complex and currently still being elucidated.

By 1980 my laboratory was recognized for working with T5 DNA polymerase, and I was invited to give talks on the subject at several places. My laboratory was the only place working on this enzyme, and I felt obligated to continue working on it even though the field was moving on to studies of eukaryotes. I gave our preparation of the enzyme to others upon request.

16-3: Fellow of Japan Society for Promotion of Sciences

The early 1980s was the period when I enjoyed the fruits of the T5 project. In 1981 I was selected as a research fellow of the Japan Society for the Promotion of Science with Dr. Yukinori Hirota as the host. I heard that Dr. Sohei Kondo, Osaka University, whom I met while he was a visiting scientist at ORNL, was instrumental in selecting me as a fellow. It was a great honor. My wife and I were in Japan for three weeks. I visited several laboratories of my former associates from my period of stay as a postdoctoral fellow at Osaka University and from former visiting scientists to ORNL.

The most memorable experience during the trip, outside of scientific activities, was meeting my former middle school teacher Kazue Kunizawa in Hofu, accompanied by my two former classmates who had come to my wedding (chapter 14). He was about eighty years old and retired after a rewarding career in oil painting. He was my homeroom teacher and art teacher at Hofu Middle

School while I attended that school, for about one year after evacuating from Manchuria (November 1946–November 1947, chapter 6). In the mid-1950s, he was approaching the retirement age of fifty-five and realized he could not afford to retire. What he did was a daring move. He quit teaching and went to Paris to study art. He got into a prestigious art contest (1957) and won. With that credential he got a contract to paint with oil, one hundred scenes in Japan, with a first-class railway pass for unlimited mileage and a free room to stay in a first-class hotel wherever he went. The paintings were exhibited at Tokyo Mitsukoshi Department Store in 1960. Mr. Kunizawa became a famous oil painter of Japanese scenes and culture. He opened an art gallery in the midst of Ginza near Wako and operated it for about twenty years. I treasure his painting of Miyajima, which he had given to me in 1947 as a gift prior to leaving for America, and the book of his oil paintings of scenes in Japan given to me at this visit. Miyajima, near Hiroshima, is considered one of the three most scenic places in Japan.

16-4: End of Phage T5 DNA Project

After I came back from Japan, I realized that research in molecular biology was definitely shifting to eukaryotes. Our funding agency, the Department of Energy, was definitely focused on research of higher eukaryotes, especially human. While Shishir Das was in my laboratory, I changed my focus to DNA polymerase in yeast, a eukaryote. I took a course on yeast at the Cold Spring Harbor Laboratory, a well-known place to take courses at the cutting edge of molecular biology, and obtained from Dr. Hartwell a mutant that I thought was the gene for a DNA polymerase. Hartwell had systematically isolated yeast mutants involved in cell division called cdc (cell division cycle) mutants and won a Nobel Prize for his studies. Based on the mutant properties, I thought cdc7 was a DNA polymerase gene, but I could not find the effect of the mutation on DNA synthesis in vitro. *Subsequently, it was found by others that cdc7 codes for a kinase that is essential for the initiation of DNA replication.*

When Shishir left I decided I should concentrate the rest of my career on T5 DNA polymerase. This wish was soon overturned. The end to the support for my T5 project came abruptly in 1984.

By then I was in a group with three other principal investigators, sharing research funds. They were Audrey Stevens, a co discoverer of RNA polymerase (circa 1960); Sankar Mitra, who also received a PhD from Paul Kaesberg at the University of Wisconsin and did postdoctoral research with Arthur Kornberg; and Salil Niyogi, who was a postdoctoral fellow of Audrey Stevens and who had subsequently married her. Salil and I shared the same laboratory. We were all transferred to the protein-engineering group headed by Fred Hartman, who at that time was also the head of the Biology Division. *Audrey was the only one among us four who was later elected to the National Academy of Sciences. Sankar may still have a chance; he is the only one among us who is still doing research full time as of this writing, at the University of Texas at Galveston. Audrey and Salil died in 2010.*

I summarized our findings on the T5 DNA polymerase at the symposium I chaired (Fujimura et al., 1981). It was also summarized by Robert Lehman (1981). The processivity and strand unwinding by a monomer of DNA polymerase were unique properties of phage T5 DNA polymerase; other well-characterized polymerases require auxiliary proteins for these functions. By 1985 we had identified the physical locus of the polymerase gene and the direction of transcription using its mutants. We had also purified and characterized the DNA binding protein of T5, which binds preferentially to the double stranded region of DNA and is essential for its replication, but the mechanism of the process is unknown. We were in the midst of attempting to isolate the clone of T5 DNA polymerase gene when I took a leave of absence to assess Japanese biotechnology (chapter17).

When I came back from the assignment, Dr. Deb Chatterjee of Life Technologies, one of the largest biochemical companies, showed interest in cloning T5 DNA polymerase. We succeeded in over-expression of the T5 DNA polymerase gene. However, Life Technologies did not commercialize it.

Many years later our findings on the fidelity and processivity of T5 DNA polymerase were confirmed with a cloned T5 DNA polymerase at Professor Charles Richardson's laboratory at Harvard (Andraos et al., 2004); Richardson is one of the most respected DNA enzymologists of my generation. They analyzed the DNA sequences that conferred processivity of replication and strand unwinding of the DNA helix.

16-5: Life with Our Children in Oak Ridge

The city was named Oak Ridge because the temporary houses were built on the ridge during the war. The main driveway stretched for miles from east to west on top of the ridge with roads coming down on the south side of the ridge to Oak Ridge Turnpike, the main highway in the valley. The roads coming down the ridge were given names of states alphabetically from the east to west, and side roads coming off these started with the same letter as the main roads. Therefore, their locations were easy to figure out. The temporary houses were built around the central section of the ridge and the roads coming down from it. These were improved into permanent structures and were still in use. After the war most of the new houses were built at the west end of the ridge, West Outer Drive, with some at the east end, East Drive. We bought a house near the east end off East Drive at Emerson Circle, built in 1957. The house was near the top of a slope. We bought it in 1965 on a thirty-year mortgage, and we built a red wood deck on the left side of the house, converted the carport to the kitchen dining area, and covered the front siding with large rocks from a riverbed just as I remembered the house in Hailar. We dwelled there until 1992, paid off the mortgage in thirty years, rented it out until 1998, and then sold it.

We have two girls, born in Oak Ridge. Tomi Chizuko was born on August 17, 1964, one year and six days after Dan. Our birthdays are one week apart—mine is July 28, Shigeko is August 4, Dan is August 11, and Tomi is August 17, only one day shorter than the pattern. Kei Eileen was the only one completely outside the pattern; she was born on February 3, 1969.

I had a second childhood while Dan was growing up. We participated in Indian Guides, Cub Scouts, and Boy Scouts, in succession, as Dan grew older. I was only a Tenderfoot Boy Scout at Opportunity, but I sat on the Scout Council as Dan went all the way to Eagle Scout. We were indebted to our neighbor David Vath, Dan's classmate, and his parents, Jim and Nancy, for Dan going all the way to an Eagle Scout. I enjoyed life with our kids. For Shigeko it was a hard life; she often considered me as another kid, which I was. Dan and Tomi were only one year apart and they kept her very busy.

She finally got help from her mother when Kei was born. Her mother was with us for about eight months; she was very sociable with our friends even though she did not speak English. We enjoyed her thoroughly; we even went to Miami with her during my professional society meetings. My colleague and I went fishing off Miami Beach, and I caught a large kingfish. Shigeko's mother made a variety of dishes for us with that fish.

The Oak Ridge school system was probably the best in the state. It was a safe place, and I was not aware of any problems. They all grew up uneventfully, although Dan had to repeat a year early in grade school.

Until Dan's problem with learning vocabulary, I assumed from my own experience that anyone who did assignments got better than average grades. He proved me wrong. A school psychologist told us that Dan lived in a dream world and was getting worse. The psychologist got hold of a doctor at Oak Ridge Associated University (ORAU), who happened to be my neighbor; his daughter was Tomi's classmate.

The doctor injected Dan's brain with the radioisotope Einsteinium, half-life 1.7 hours, as a tracer to check blood circulation in the brain. He did not find anything wrong. The half-life of the isotope was so short that I did not feel there was any danger of it causing an ill effect. I was using a radioisotope as a tracer in my own experiments with bacteria, so I thought it was just a routine procedure. *Many years later the same doctor was on national TV accused of using radioisotopes in experiments on humans without proper permission. I recognized him as the doctor that injected the isotope into the brain of our son. I was surprised that Dan was one of his experimental subjects.*

I think Dan inherited his traits from me. Shigeko agrees that I lived in a dream world in Oak Ridge. I lived in an ivory tower where I carried out research the way I wanted, which was fishing for something that aroused my curiosity. Then I investigated it by doing experiments. I initiated and planned my own projects and worked at my own pace without any pressure. I published when I felt I had some unique findings.

I attributed Dan's learning problems to language. Just prior to starting school, Shigeko and our three children were in Japan for a few months, and the children's primary language had changed to Japanese. Dan did not have time to convert back to English prior to going to school and had problems learning English vocabulary. I was too preoccupied with my research to help him. He received special help from two of his teachers, Mrs. Hagen and Mrs. Oakberg. They were conscientious teachers and tried various ways for him to learn vocabulary and to read.

Shigeko took our children to Japan occasionally, and her mother came to the States three times. Our children were close to her; there appeared to be no communication problems, even though our children did not know much Japanese. They learned more Japanese after leaving Oak Ridge (chapter 25).

While the children were growing up, we went on a day hike to the Smoky Mountains National Park or Cumberland Mountains. I think we did all the day hike trails in the Smoky Mountains that we found in a guidebook.

We traveled a lot, driving with a tent in our Oldsmobile station wagon. We went to all forty-eight lower states and most of the Canadian provinces, occasionally as side trips to my professional meetings. Camping along the way provided memorable experiences. Morning breakfasts at campsites were a very refreshing way to start a day. One time it was raining during the night, and when I looked out of the tent, the tent was surrounded by water.

One incident I thought was funny was the time we camped off Blue Ridge Parkway. We met the family of a former Oak Ridger who had moved to North Carolina. Our old-style Coleman ice chest with a metal hook was loaded with meats and vegetables. During the night a bear showed up and dragged the chest about a hundred yards, opened it, and took everything except the seaweed and onions. My wife was trembling, and I was sound asleep. Several years later we were camping at a site in Yellowstone. A ranger gathered us and told us that the food kept in ice chests with metal hooks is safe. However, she said she heard that bears in the Smoky Mountains are smart; they know how to unhook the ice chests. I was surprised; apparently, this was a well-known fact among the rangers. Another precaution, told to me by my colleague at the lab, was to never have smoked meat in the chest and to never keep it in the car. A bear would scratch the car trying to get in. Instead the ice chest should be kept hanging from a tree branch.

Our children participated in a foreign exchange student program while they were in their junior or senior high school. Dan went to Guatemala. Soon after he came back, the father of his partner was assassinated. Dan told me the boy's father was always carrying a gun, but he was killed in a case of mistaken identity. An alternate boy came to stay with us, who did not speak a word of English. However, we enjoyed the boy and took him to Mammoth Cave. Tomi's counterpart was from Stockholm, Sweden. Her mother came for a few days and did not like her daughter sleeping on a bunk bed, but that was the only bed available. Tomi had a good time in Stockholm. Kei's partner was from Normandy, France; they had happy experiences both in France and Oak Ridge. A summer soon afterward, our family stayed in Malaga, Spain, for a week, and Kei stayed on for the rest of the summer, going around Europe with a backpack. I guess we were brave to let her do it. I think most parents of a girl that age would not let her do it.

16-6: Social Life in Oak Ridge

Initially, we centered our social activities on Volkin's group and their spouses. We had parties often at one or other private homes. Shigeko was a wonderful hostess and cook. We had guests, sometimes as many as about fifty at one time. On one such occasion, I made tempura, deep-fried vegetables and shrimps coated with thin dough, at the kitchen counter for four persons at a time all night long.

For the first few years of our stay, Oak Ridge was dry; we had to go to Knoxville to buy liquor. We bought liquor by the case because we had parties at homes and took a bottle to a restaurant, where it provided us with a setup. We drank more during the dry era than after the city became wet. After that we had fewer parties at homes, and at restaurants liquor was served by the drink, which was more expensive.

Shigeko was more outgoing and became a friend of the spouses of Japanese visiting scientists, most of whom were physicists and engineers at ORNL located at X-10 and MDs at Oak Ridge Associated University. When I joined the laboratory, there was a visiting scientist, Dr. M. Yoneda, from Takeda Pharmaceutical at Fred Bollum's laboratory on the same floor. While at Bollum laboratory, he discovered an enzyme that added nucleotides at an end of the DNA chain; it is widely used even today. Through Yoneda I met other visiting Japanese scientists in the Biology Division including Dr. Sohei Kondo. Kondo was a theoretical physicist, but the occupational force had forbidden him to work on his profession. Therefore, he became a biophysicist; he was a visiting scientist, an expert in radiation dosimetry.

Dr. Tsuneo Yamada was another well-known Japanese scientist; he was a group leader in the division. He was famous for studies on the development of lizards. Prior to the Japanese defeat, he was in the best engineering corps of the Japanese Army. Prior to the war, his corps was in Manchuria clearing jungles near the border with Siberia; the Japanese were planning to invade Siberia. When the US government stopped exporting oil to Japan, their plan had changed to the Pacific. Then his corps was sent to Rabaul, New Britain, off the coast of Australia, to build an airfield for the Japanese. It served as a base for the battles around the Solomon Islands. He told me about a stupid act of the base commander. A shipment of new planes arrived on the base. He gave orders to have a ceremony to celebrate their arrival and lined up all the planes on the field. American planes came in for the raid and destroyed all of them. While still at Rabaul, Yamada got amoebic dysentery and was sent back to Japan on a hospital ship; thus his life was saved because the transport ship carrying the rest of the corps to a new assignment sank.

Another wartime episode, I got from a visiting scientist who was in a Japanese tank battalion. He told me he was in the best Japanese tank battalion. Its tanks were all captured from the British at Singapore.

Frequently, we took these visitors and other guests hiking and picnicking into the Smoky Mountains with our children. During the years of our life in Oak Ridge, the visiting scientists and their children got younger than us as the older guests left and newer ones came. An incident I remember was a hike with a visiting physicist who was older than the local friends. He claimed he was an expert on mushrooms. We went picking mushrooms with him several times. We trusted him and ate whatever he said was safe. He said all the mushrooms with sponge-like patterns underneath their cups were nonpoisonous, but one of mushrooms *was* poisonous only when we had an alcoholic drink with it. We even found one matsutake, a Japanese delicacy. Many years later another visiting scientist told me that the self-claimed expert on mushrooms did not know much. We were lucky that none of us got sick! Even that matsutake was suspect; we never found another one during our stay in Oak Ridge, almost thirty years.

For a period I was on the board of the Oak Ridge Chamber Music Association and had a party for visiting musicians at our home a few times—some of them were quite famous. We got these performers at the beginning of their fame so that they were not too expensive. These included Ms. Ushioda Makiko, a violinist, and a Tokyo quartet. We hosted these performers after their respective concerts. The Japanese performers tended to get their fame overseas first, and then they became recognized within Japan. Perhaps the most famous performer at the concerts we attended was Isaac Stern, a violinist.

He was a classmate of Dr. Waldo Cohn at the University of California at Berkeley. Waldo was a biochemist at the Biology Division. He was a self-taught cellist who used to play music with Isaac Stern while at the university.

Waldo Cohn received PhD (1938) for using ^{32}P as a tracer to study metabolism of phosphorus in rats. The phosphorus radioisotope, ^{32}P, was isolated from the Berkeley cyclotron. He was a participant of the Manhattan project in Chicago in 1942 and studied the metabolism of fission products. He moved to Oak Ridge in 1943. He developed the ion exchange column to fractionate fission products. He applied this technique to fractionate and purify all the nucleosides and nucleotides, monomers of DNA and RNA polymers; he found one new nucleoside present in transfer RNA, pseudouridine. When I was on a special assignment in 1985–1986 to Japan (chapter 17), I was surprised to see, outdoor at one of biotechnology companies, two huge ion exchange columns for separating nucleotides; they credited Waldo Cohn for the development of the technique. They market purine nucleotides as an essence of taste. It puzzles me to this day why Waldo Cohn was not elected to the National Academy of Sciences.

Waldo was also recognized as the authority on nomenclatures in life sciences; he served as the director of the Office of Biochemical Nomenclature (1965–1976). He made scientists adhere strictly to the guidelines, which he helped establish. I always made sure that he edited my papers prior to submission for publication. I depended on him and our floor secretary to edit and proofread my papers. Therefore, I did not proofread my papers until I left the division. It has remained my weakness to this day.

Waldo was the first conductor of the Oak Ridge Symphony Orchestra, served for eleven years, and was its cellist until a year before he died in 1999. Oak Ridge Orchestra is the oldest continuously existing orchestra in Tennessee. Many of its performers were also scientists at ORNL. Its pianist, who performed solo occasionally, was Dr. Ralph Einstein, my associate at the Biology Division. He was our X-ray crystallographer but was good enough to be a concert pianist. He chose to be a scientist but was better known in the community as a pianist.

Waldo was also the first mayor of Oak Ridge. He integrated blacks into the Oak Ridge school system and was almost impeached for his action. It was shocking that the city established by the government had a segregated village for the blacks, and they were segregated even in the laboratory. The laboratory had separate restrooms for blacks and whites. By the time we came in 1963, there was no overt segregation. Even though the black village still existed, some blacks had houses throughout the city. The Biology Division had the integrated annual division dance party; the division was the first one to integrate dance parties, even prior to our arrival.

The one and only community project I participated in throughout my stay in Oak Ridge was to play in the city tennis leagues. The city had its tennis leagues divided into two seasons. At its height of popularity, it had more than thirty leagues categorized based on skill with eleven players per league. We played one game per week, and at the end of each half of the season, the top player of each league received a trophy.

I did not play regularly outside of the league matches and was not very competitive. I usually played in a single's league, and sometimes I played in double and mixed double leagues but only when I was asked to be a partner. Near the end of our stay in Oak Ridge, I finally won the championships in the single's league twice—the summers of 1987 and 1988 in leagues eleven and ten, respectively. I think these were about the middle-ranked leagues. In 1989 I got an excellent partner, a student of a friend and colleague, Waldy Generoso. We won the championship in team tennis. Waldy's wife, Estella, and I teamed up several times for a mixed double, but we never won a championship.

Waldy was an excellent player. He started to play with me but was a more serious player. He was practicing with his son, who is my son's age, in the middle of the hot summer, staying on the court for hours. Before I became aware, he was near the top of the leagues. He has so many trophies covering his shelves that I never counted. Some of those in the top league played in the statewide tournament. I appreciated those players that organized the tournament year after year, almost from the beginning of the city.

Annual fishing trips we had with about six colleagues at the Biology Division were very memorable events in the mid-sixties to mid-seventies; they were usually organized by Charlie Mead. We went to the North and South Carolina coast of the Atlantic Ocean or the Gulf of Mexico

141

in the Florida panhandle. We went on a party boat and caught a huge number of a variety of fish—dolphinfish, tuna, bonito, mackerel, wahoo, red snapper, grouper, and some others. Our catches decreased year after year. The last trip we made was on a charter boat—Charlie Mead, Gary Vandenvos, and me with our spouses in October 12, 1974. Each of us caught a marlin; Charlie got the largest, a 240-pound and eleven-foot-long blue marlin. I got the smallest, a six-foot-one-eighth inch white marlin. *I was the only one who had it mounted; ever since then it has been displayed prominently in our living room.* We took back the blue marlin by freezing it overnight and wrapping it in sleeping bags. Charlie drove his full-size van. The eleven-foot blue marlin had its nose and tail sticking out from the sleeping bags and car. We stopped at a gas station, and people gathered around and poked at the midsection of the bag to see if it was really that big. Charlie left it in his driveway all night long to thaw.

The next evening we invited everyone at the Biology Division to the laboratory-owned park that had a large grill under shade. We barbecued the marlin in several ways and had some raw—sashimi. It was the last fishing trip we went on organized by Volkin's group. We had some leftover fish in our car trunk and left it there overnight; I forgot to put it in our refrigerator. The next day Shigeko had some Japanese housewives over and had sashimi. Apparently, it was still fresh; they enjoyed eating it.

Charlie left the head of his blue marlin in the lab freezer for a long time and was going to mount it someday but never did. I do not remember what Gary did with his white marlin. We were one of many boats that went out from Destin, Florida, that day, and our boat got three out of the six marlins that were caught.

Subsequently, four of us from the Biology Division, with our families, rented a house for a week for a few summers at Edisto Island, South Carolina. Waldy Generoso organized the trips. Each family was from a different ethnicity; I do not think it was done consciously, but I realized it as I wrote this. We did crabbing, clam digging, and fishing. We got crabs using a couple of traps made from chicken wire with chicken necks inside. We got clams by squatting in the shallow water and sticking our hands into the sandy bottom. I stood for hours in the water with a fishing rod. The only thing I remember was that I caught mostly small catfish. We had feasts of crabs and clams. When we first went to Edisto Island, there were only beach houses, but the last time we were there, there were motels and shopping malls. I liked going to the Outer Banks in North Carolina, just with my family, perhaps because there were spots with hardly anyone or any buildings around. We enjoyed fishing and walking along the shore.

PART IV:

A MOLECULAR BIOLOGIST IN COLLABORATIVE PROJECTS

CHAPTER 17:
DIPLOMATIC ASSIGNMENT TO JAPAN

One day in 1984, I received a phone call from Dr. Al Hellman of the US Commerce Department. He asked if I knew someone who was bicultural and bilingual in Japanese and English. I said I did not know, and then I realized I was. Al was a visiting scientist at the Biology Division of ORNL in the early 60s and talked to Dr. Richard Griesemer, our previous division director. He suggested me. Al was looking for someone to send to Japan to assess the progress of biotechnology in Japan and other countries in the Far East. I was thinking of doing some duty for our government in return for the wonderful life I had been having in the United States. I accepted. My counterpart in Europe was Dr. Robert Yuan, a son of a former diplomat of China. He had experienced living in several countries around the world as a family member of a diplomat. He was suave and accustomed to talking to strangers.

I was the extreme opposite. I became a scientist because I wanted to have minimal interactions with people. I almost never initiated a conversation even one-on-one. Now I would have to initiate interacting with others by visiting them. This was a completely new experience for me, and Al Hellman noticed it and was probably perturbed. Initially, we went around biotechnology companies in the United States, most of them newly created. Bob Yuan initiated conversation at these meetings. After doing that for a few months, I took a leave of absence from ORNL. Our director at Department of Energy (DOE) had told me that it would be the end to my research career because when I come back, I would not get independent funding to do research. I was very naïve; when Al asked how much I was getting, I only mentioned my net pay at ORNL and accepted only the net amount. Al noted that it was very low. Later, I learned that I should have included all my benefits including the additional amount I was getting for my savings plan from the company. I never asked for a raise throughout my career. I accepted whatever was offered.

We moved to Washington, DC to take orientation courses on diplomatic etiquette and the history of the United States and Japan. Professors from Georgetown University taught us these courses. The professor on the history of the United States said there is no good history book available; perhaps the best one is *Chesapeake,* a novel by James Michener. Brenda Underwood, a former assistant to Salil Niyogi, who had moved to the National Institute of Cancer, had a copy of the book. I borrowed it and took it to Japan to finish reading. I enjoyed it just as I did all of Michener's books I read.

The professor on Japanese history said that near the end of World War II, the Russians overran Manchuria. I told him that was not true, that I lived in Qiqihar at the end of the war, and the Russians did not come until at least a week after the war. I told him that he needed to do more research prior to teaching about Manchuria.

As for etiquette we were told we should always be at a party prior to the arrival of the ambassador and to make sure someone was always engaged in conversation with him. I did not attend any such parties.

I was sworn in as a secretary (Photo 17). I was posted to the American Embassy in Tokyo in September 1985 for fourteen months. We stayed on the eighth floor of the Harris Tower of

Photo 17: Pledging that I would faithfully serve as a member of the US Foreign Service.

the embassy apartment complex in Roppongi. We had a view of Mount Fuji on a clear day from one of the windows. Our unit was on two floors—one floor had the living room and kitchen and another floor had two bedrooms. My wife said she felt like she was in heaven living in the embassy compound in the middle of Tokyo. She had easy access to Japanese culture and cuisine yet lived in a condominium of the American standard. It was quite a change from a small town deep in the mountains of Tennessee.

During my appointment I traveled extensively in Hokkaido, Honshu, and Kyushu. However, originally, I was supposed to go to other countries in the Far East, but I did not go because of insufficient funds. I did not come back to the States at all and felt isolated. Instead, I traveled extensively within Japan. According to my records, I talked with thirty-eight national and prefectural government bureaucrats, twenty-eight professors of universities, twenty-seven directors of academic and national research laboratories, and fifty-one executives and research directors of private biotechnology companies.

The year I began to assess Japanese biotechnology (1985) was considered year one of the new age of biotechnology in Japan by Nikkei Biotechnology, a major newspaper of the field. Biotechnology companies included those that produce traditional Japanese fermented foods such as soy sauce and miso made from fermented soybeans. When I went to a soy sauce manufacturer in Kyushu, I was surprised to learn that he knew of Kanaya miso in Hofu, which was my father's family business for more than a century.

Modern food companies produce and market purified fermentation products. Ajinomoto is well known for producing and marketing monosodium glutamate as an "essence of taste." Kyowa Hakko is the largest producer of ethanol and its derivatives. It produced most of the ethanol used to blend with sake. Meiji Seika, a confectionery company, produced penicillin soon after World War II and marketed kanamycin, the first antibiotic developed in Japan. At the time of my visit, it was the only company producing penicillin and streptomycin in Japan.

The major biotechnology products of global interest are pharmaceuticals. Takeda Pharmaceutical is a global pharmaceutical company, fifteenth in the world. *Its annual sales increased from $2 billion in 1985 to $806 billion in 2010. It has research and development (R&D) laboratories not only in Japan but also in the United States, Europe, and Asia trying to develop therapeutics for obesity, diabetes, atherosclerosis, cancer, and diseases of the central nervous system. It markets its products in more than one hundred countries. It corroborates with academia and other pharmaceutical and biotechnology companies. During my assignment in 1986, several Japanese companies told me that a promising biotech company in America was Amgen. Takeda acquired it in 2008.*

Another pharmaceutical company that is doing research and development using recombinant DNA technologies is Shionogi Pharmaceuticals. A staff member at the embassy told me that it has a close relationship with Eli Lilly. It was marketing recombinant DNA-derived insulin developed by Eli Lilly. It has laboratories in Japan and the United States and has joint ventures with other US companies. *It acquired Sciele Pharma Inc, Atlanta GA, in 2008. It has diversified, and the annual sales in 2010 were $2 billion.*

As shown by these two examples, pharmaceutical companies and others in food and chemicals stayed competitive by doing research and development in collaboration with academia and commercial companies, not only domestically but also in America and Europe, and by acquisition of smaller biotechnology companies with promising products. Their goal is to survive by becoming global companies by joint ventures, acquisitions, and mergers; in-house R&D is not sufficient.

One of the goals of my assignment was to assess the impact of the Ministry of International Trade and Industry (MITI) directed projects in biotechnology, specifically, in the development of technologies involved in bioreactors, large-scale mammalian cell cultures, recombinant DNAs, functional protein systems, and bioelectronic devices. The MITI's purpose was to induce collaboration among commercial companies, but my impression from the views expressed by the administrators of several participating companies was that they did not expect significant findings; they were nominally involved just to keep the government bureaucrats satisfied. My subsequent observation is that each individual company has its own R&D programs and gets involved in joint ventures with specific companies and is not serious about a group project such as that of MITI. The reputation of farsighted visions by MITI is exaggerated.

During my assignment, I sent cables to several officers in the US government describing my findings that are relevant to biotechnology (this was prior to e-mail becoming common). I sent twenty-seven cables during my fourteen months' stay. By the end of the tenure, I felt I knew about Japan and her people more than most of the Japanese. My reports on biotechnology in Japan were published by the National Technical Information Service, US Department of Commerce (1988, 1989). The latter publication reported on the activities at several specific companies. The director of the National Institute of General Medical Sciences told me that my reports are the bible of Japanese biotechnology.

I perceived that science and technology areas that would make great contributions are drug design and nanotechnology. I observed an investigator at a pharmaceutical company who was busy designing a drug by computer modeling. However, proteins have many possible ways of folding, and the theory for it is incomplete. We need better understanding of the structure of a protein essential for interaction with a specific target. *Recent advances in mass spectrometry makes it possible to finally assay peptides synthesized for specific targets such as a specific pathologic organism. This methodology, known as targeted proteomics, was selected as the Method of the Year 2012 by* Nature Methods, *January 2013. Synthetic peptide targeted to interact with a specific molecule of an organism would be more specific than any antibody and could be developed much faster by targeted proteomics.*

Another is nanotechnology. I heard the term for the first time from an investigator at one of the laboratories. It is to design devices at atomic levels. Its potential application is huge in fields such as artificial intelligence, medical devices, sensors, and receptors. *Nanotechnology has finally become an everyday word, and devices based on its principles are being developed. A hope of this century is to solve many apparent intractable problems by its applications.*

The embassy compound had excellent tennis courts and a swimming pool. I kept up my tennis skills by frequently playing with one of the Japanese staff at the embassy. I sometimes played with my Japanese scientific colleagues. I even played once with a daughter of my former classmate Hatsunori Sasaki at Hofu Middle School. She was then a student at a college in Tokyo.

One aspect of embassy funding that surprised me was that they had funds to improve the tennis courts and swimming pool but did not have funds for consulate officers to visit the embassy at Tokyo. They had to come at their own expense. Apparently, their budgets came from different sources.

My assignment came at the right time for my personal affairs. We invited Uncle and Aunt Yoshiwada along with some cousins to a Thanksgiving dinner to express my gratitude for all they had done in the past. We drove Shigeko's father around the vicinity of Tokyo. That was the one and only one time I went sightseeing with him. During my visit to the Kyowa Hakko Laboratory in Hofu, I was able to see Uncle and Aunt Kawamura. During my assignment was the last time I saw these relatives. They passed away soon after we left Japan.

CHAPTER 18:
MOUSE GENETICS

When I came back to the Biology Division at ORNL, I was shocked to find that the budget situation was in terrible shape; the budget was decreasing year by year. If Hartman had told me of the situation, I could have remained in Japan at another position doing similar work assessing Japanese biotechnology; I had rejected the offer for such a position instantly without giving it a thought. I wanted to go back to the Biology Division. However, as soon as I got back, I realized I no longer belonged to the Biology Division. I felt like I was hanging from a cliff, holding desperately by a finger.

The mouse section had some extra funds, and Waldy Generoso got me interested in working on chemical induction of mutagenesis in mice.I joined his project as a collaborator. I sacrificed many mice by cervical dislocation to get at their embryos to get their DNA to analyze excision and reinsertion of retroviruses induced by chemical mutagens. Multiple copies of retroviruses are integrated in mouse genomic DNA, and its translocation was analyzed by treatment with restriction enzymes. A restriction enzyme cuts DNA at a specific sequence yielding characteristic DNA fragments from a genome; the method is known as "restriction fragment length polymorphism" (RFLP). These DNA fragments were fractionated by size by gel electrophoresis yielding DNA fragment profiles unique for each species of mice. When the profile has changed, it is an indication that the DNA sequence has changed due to excision and reinsertion of a retrovirus.

We analyzed 324 embryos and observed four new locations of provirus in mouse genomes induced by the exposure of their mothers to ethyl methanesulfonate, a mutagenic chemical. We decided that it was not significant enough for publication and never submitted. However, a few years later, a researcher on mutagenesis told me that the finding was significant and should have been published. By then I had left Oak Ridge.

My research life in the Biology Division was rapidly coming to an end. The research budget of the division kept on shrinking. My project with Generoso was having problems getting external funding. Near the end of 1990, they had a voluntary reduction in force. I took it, retired, and became a consultant, thinking I should be able to find a job utilizing my knowledge on Japanese biotechnology.

I spent the best period of my research career at the Biology Division Oak Ridge National Laboratory

156

(1963–1990). It was my ivory tower where I spent most of the time doing basic research on my own projects, planned and performed at my pace without any pressure to publish. I gradually overcame my shyness and got involved in teaching laboratory techniques to graduate and undergraduate students and taught the course on molecular biology of DNA for several years and served on the committees of the Biology Division and the University of Tennessee graduate school at Oak Ridge. I produced one PhD and started to interact with well-established scientists to tell them of our findings.

Socially, I was also becoming more expressive of my thoughts and experiences. My social life gradually changed from scientific and Japanese communities to church communities. My views on church and religion are expressed in detail in Part V.

CHAPTER 19:
FOOD AND DRUG ADMINISTRATION

My work as a consultant on Japanese biotechnology was not doing very well. I was giving information for free. I received compensation only once, and I received it because I was not involved in the dealing.

The opportunity for a new direction in my profession came rather unexpectedly and suddenly. In the Christmas card for 1991, Larry Bockstahler, my contemporary at Kaesberg's laboratory, asked me if I would be interested in joining him in a collaborative project. He has a laboratory at the Food and Drug Administration (FDA) in Rockville, Maryland, near Washington, DC. I expressed interest thinking that a position at the FDA would give me opportunities to look for a position in the government or a biotechnology company in the area. Larry suggested that I try to get a senior fellowship from the National Research Council (NRC) to work at his laboratory in Rockville. I immediately applied for the fellowship and received it; the appointment was for two years, starting June 1, 1992.

We rented out our house in which we lived for about twenty-five years, thinking we might return after the appointment. We left enough furniture to rent our house as furnished. This was a mistake. We lost most of the furniture and toys that had any value; the renters of the house took them when they moved out. We settled in a townhouse in Rockville near the laboratory. I immediately started to work at Larry's laboratory.

Larry obtained from his colleague in Germany brain tissues from several regions of the brain of two AIDS patients—one with neuropathological symptoms and another without. My project was to quantify HIV DNA in these brain tissues by the polymerase chain reaction (PCR) technique. It was an application of methods I used in my research on DNA replication *in vitro*. The PCR technique amplifies the number of copies of DNA manyfold. The public became familiar with the technique from the movie based on the book *Jurassic Park* by J. Michael Crichton and the O. J. Simpson murder trial. It is now routinely used to identify a person from a minute quantity of body parts and fluids.

Our analysis suggested that the distribution of HIV DNA in the brain was not uniform and was highest in the hippocampus of both cases. I gave a seminar on my findings at Robert Gallo's laboratory at the NIH; Gallo was the codiscoverer of HIV as the cause of AIDS.

I went occasionally to Johns Hopkins Medical School to participate in the seminars on the neuropathology of

AIDS at Dr. Richard Johnson's laboratory. He was one of the recognized authorities in the field, and the seminars gave me information about the current trends in the field.

We enjoyed the culture in Washington, DC. We went to see exhibits at the Smithsonian frequently. We enjoyed the concerts at Lincoln Center and Japanese arts, music, and lectures at the Japan Culture Center sponsored by the Japanese Embassy. The lectures at the culture center were new experiences. I actively asked questions. One of the responses I got that I paraphrased occasionally is the one given by a Buddhist monk. I do not remember my question, but he replied that humans are incapable of learning absolute truth. I was surprised at a religious person saying that, but I agree. Everything we perceive is an interpretation by our brain. At the end of each event at the culture center, they served sushi for free.

The service of significance I did for the Department of Energy and the National institute of Health during that period was to go to Japan with a group of scientists to assess protein engineering research in Japan, November 6–14 of 1992. The report submitted by the group stated that the methodologies and apparatus were state-of-the-art but the projects lacked originality. However, from my previous experiences, I would say that they do not talk to visitors about research projects with originality; in my opinion, they are as original as American research laboratories.

We visited three top universities—Tokyo, Osaka, and Kyoto Universities—but concluded that they have substandard facilities compared to equivalent US institutions. Their funds and space are much smaller. The Institute for Protein Research at Osaka University was the only academic institution with facilities equivalent to those found in the industry and government laboratories. I went there as a postdoctoral fellow for a year (1961–1962) (chapter 13). Its facilities may be better than American state universities.

We visited four industrial laboratories—Kirin Brewery Central Laboratories for Key Technology, Mitsubishi Kasei Central Research Department, Suntory Institute for Biomedical Research, and Yamanouchi Pharmaceutical. They have state-of-the-art facilities with long-range goals. Their researchers are lifetime employees and permitted to go to university laboratories to learn new technologies (including overseas). This may be the reason their goals appeared to have longer ranges than that of American counterparts.

We visited the Protein Engineering Research Institute (PERI) as an example of the government laboratories. It is relatively new and established to enhance basic research relevant to protein engineering and to promote a multidisciplinary environment for training industrial scientists. The attitudes of industrial laboratory managers were similar to what I had perceived during my previous visit in 1985 to 1986 for MITI organized projects. They do not expect much from these projects, but to avoid antagonizing MITI bureaucrats, they participate in the projects. Even when a researcher found something new, the researcher kept it a secret and took it back to his or her own laboratory. The report of our study team was submitted to sponsored institutions and labeled "for administrative use only."

Near the end of my appointment at the FDA in 1995, Dr. Nobuyuki Nishimura, a former guest scientist at the Biology Division, ORNL, invited me as a guest professor to Toho University, Chiba, for a week. I gave five lectures in five days (January 9–13): (1)Quantitative Determination of HIV DNA in Brain Tissues of AIDS Patients; (2) Societal Impacts of Gene Manipulation; (3) Overview of AIDS Research; (4) Mechanisms of DNA Polymerase; and (5) Polymerase Chain Reaction Techniques. I covered all the projects I was involved in for the previous ten years.

We spent an additional two weeks in Tokyo, Mishima, and Nishinomiya (January 15–30). We were in Tokyo at the time of the Great Hanshin Earthquake (January 17). That early morning I was jogging around the Tokyo municipal government buildings, near the time-share hotel where we were staying, and felt the earth shaking. Tokyo was shaking frequently, and I did not think much about it. I came back to our room and was surprised to learn from the TV that there was a major earthquake near Kobe almost four hundred miles away. That morning I gave a lecture on my project at Tokyo University Medical Research Institute, and when I came back, I was shocked to see on TV that Kobe was a sea of fire.

On the way to Kansai, we stopped over a couple of days in Mishima, and I gave a lecture to young scientists at the National Institute of Genetics on my views on scientific research in Japanese and American graduate schools. In Kansai we stayed at Shigeko's sister Noriko Abe's home in Senriyama near Nishinomiya. I walked around Kobe and looked at the houses squashed by the quake. People were walking around with backpacks. The scene reminded me of the major cities in Japan after the war.

During our stay in Rockville, I played tennis regularly with Jim Strickland. He was a much better player than I was. He was in Oak Ridge for a while as a postdoctoral fellow of Bruce Jacobson, and he was in a higher city league (chapter 16-6). Soon after I joined Larry Bockstahler's laboratory, I saw a familiar face of a woman at a nearby laboratory. I recognized that she was the wife of Jim. Thus, we were reacquainted. He became my valuable friend. He was a computer expert at one of the laboratories at the NIH and willingly gave me advice whenever I had a computer problem. Another surprise was that he worked next to Ulrike Lichti, my peer and a female friend while on the third floor of the biochemistry building at the University of Wisconsin. She was also Larry Bockstahler's friend from the Wisconsin era. They are both German origin and probably close friends. We socialized a few times.

We would have enjoyed our stay in the DC area, but I could not find a job I liked. I was offered a position at a laboratory of the FDA on the NIH campus and at Howard University Medical School. I declined both; I still wanted to continue research on HIV-associated dementia by the approach I was taking.

CHAPTER 20:
DEPARTMENT OF PSYCHIATRY AND BEHAVIORAL SCIENCES, UNIVERSITY OF MIAMI

One day I met Dr. Ljubisa Vikovic, an officer at the AIDS office at the National Institute of Mental Health, while walking nearby his building and gave him the progress report on my project. He showed interest in my findings and promised to provide me with a grant to continue on my project if I could find a position. I wrote to Dr. Paul Shapshak at the University of Miami School of Medicine about the possibility of my going to his laboratory. I met Shapshak while he was at NIH for a grant-study group meeting (March 13, 1995). His talk was similar to my interests, and I had talked to him about my project. He replied promptly that he was very much interested. He got me an appointment at the Department of Psychiatry and Behavioral Science where he has his laboratory. It is the same school as that of Dr. Antero So, whom I invited to the Biology Division symposium, which I chaired about fifteen years earlier (chapter 15). He was a professor in the biochemistry department there. I met him after I got there; he was surprised to see me, treated me to a lunch, and mentioned that he could have gotten me a position in the biochemistry department. I regularly attended its departmental seminars to keep up with the development in molecular biology/biochemistry.

My project at Shapshak's laboratory was to correlate HIV-1 DNA and RNA load in several regions of the brain to the severity of HIV-1-associated dementia. I used PCR to quantify viral DNA and RNA (June, 1995–July, 2001). My contributions to the project were summarized in *Neuro-AIDS* (2006).

Paul Shapshak had about ten students, postdoctoral fellows, and associates working in his laboratory. We collaborated with Dr. Karl Goodkin of the department and Dr. Carol Petito of the pathology department on our project.

Our results suggested that HIV-1 proviral DNA load in the medial temporal lobe, which included the hippocampus, is significantly better related to the severity of HIV-associated dementia than in the frontal lobe, basal ganglia or the medial temporal lobe without the hippocampus. Therefore, the HIV-1 load in the hippocampus may have impaired the cognition. Proviral DNA in the infected brain tissues is an archive of HIV-1 that had infected the brain of a deceased patient. Proviral DNA is integrated in the host chromosomes, and only a fraction of these may have been transcribed into RNA and present in a specimen. These RNAs are spliced into monogenomic sequences (multispliced RNA) prior to translation into proteins. The multispliced RNA is continuously degraded. Therefore, only the actively transcribed ones at the time of death were present in the autopsied specimen. RNA in viral particles is the complete genomic size (unspliced RNA). These are infectious agents that are transmitted to other cells and regions and are stably present in the brain. The ratio of these two types of RNAs would indicate how active the viral genomes were at the time of death. Our results suggested that the expression of viral genome was most active in the frontal lobe.

We had funding problems and rapidly lost workers in the laboratory. I withdrew from his laboratory in 2001 and got into a project on Alzheimer's disease at a laboratory in the Veterans Hospital.

CHAPTER 21:
VETERANS AFFAIRS MEDICAL CENTER IN MIAMI

By 2001 I realized that we had sufficient income from my pension, investments, and social security, so I could carry on research as a volunteer without pay. Professor Carl Eisdorfer, chairman of the psychiatry department, was trying to get me to do research on Alzheimer's disease and introduced me to Dr. Bernard Roos, the director of Geriatric Research, Education, and Clinical Center, Veterans Hospital (GRECC, VAMC) situated adjacent to the University of Miami's medical school. He had extra funds to do exploratory projects. I made a proposal to analyze changes in the expression of genes relevant to cognition and memory in the hippocampus of Alzheimer's disease cases using PCR. He accepted me and added me to Dr. Guy Howard's laboratory (January, 2002). Professor Carol Petito introduced me to

Dr. Dennis Dickson, Mayo Clinic, Jacksonville, Florida. He managed the tissue bank where human brains were housed for Alzheimer's disease cases. I received a support for the reagents for the project, a laboratory space, and all the necessary facilities. Dr. Petito had introduced me to laser-capture microdissection of neurons, and her assistant taught me how to use it. I later got access to the shared instrument at the Imaging Laboratory, Diabetes Research Institute, University of Miami School of Medicine, which was accessible almost anytime I needed it, and a technician was there to deal with any problems I may have with the instrument. Dr. Carlos Perez-Stable and Teresita Reiner, colleagues at GRECC, also joined the project. They were experts in double immunofluorescence microscopy that would specifically differentiate cells containing two agents.

We tested the hypothesis that the accumulation of amyloid beta peptides and neurofibrillary tangles made from tau proteins in neurons cause Alzheimer's disease. Amyloid beta peptide is formed by degradation of its precursor protein; its function is not known. In the normal brain, these peptides are removed, but in Alzheimer's disease they accumulate as extra cellular plaques. Tau proteins are constituents of microtubules, which when hyperphosphorylated aggregate into neurofibrillary tangles. The genes I chose were brain-derived neurotrophic factor (BDNF), which is involved in memory and cognition; dynamine I (DYN), which is involved in acquisition of memory; and cytochrome C oxidase subunit II (COX2),which is a mitochondria gene involved in energy production. We compared changes in the expression of these genes in neurons associated with amyloid beta peptides and those neurons free of these peptides. Our results showed that the expression of BDNF and DYN are reduced in neurons from Alzheimer's disease, but the association with amyloid beta peptides is not obligatory. Double immunofluorescence microscopy yielded consistent results that these genes are expressed even in the presence of amyloid beta peptides or hyperphosphorylated tau proteins (Fujimura, et al., 2010).

This is still a controversial issue; there are investigators pursuing research to prevent plaques and neurofibrillary tangle formation as a way to prevent Alzheimer's disease. Alzheimer's disease may have multiple causes, and the prevention of plaques and tangles may cure some of them. I included a mitochondria protein because there is a hypothesis that oxidative stress causes Alzheimer's disease. Oxidative stress is caused by the dysfunction of mitochondria, which causes reduction of COX2 expression. The effect of Alzheimer's disease on COX2 expression differed case by case and appeared not to have any correlative effect.

CHAPTER 22:
SOCIAL LIFE IN MIAMI

In 1997 we bought a house in Miami surrounded by palm trees and tropical bushes. It had a big swimming pool and a Jacuzzi connected by a small waterfall. While we were still kids in Opportunity, I promised Jerry I would live in a house with a swimming pool and tennis court. I accomplished at least one of my promises. We bought the house even though the support for my research was uncertain. We hoped to stay and enjoy the place as long as both of us were healthy.

We called the Jacuzzi *onsen*, which is the Japanese word for hot spring bath. It was the major attraction for our house guests. We did not swim much, but we heated the Jacuzzi at least one night a week. Fireflies would fly around as we soaked. It made us relax physically and mentally. Every Saturday morning Shigeko taught Japanese kindergarten at the school for Japanese children to keep up on the Japanese language and came home exhausted. Taking onsen just before going to bed was a perfect way to relax.

She enjoyed teaching these kids; she fulfilled her dream of getting back to her profession whenever she got a chance. She thinks kindergarten is the most important period for the development of the social and psychological well-being of a person.

We had houseguests frequently. They were our children, my siblings, our relatives, and friends from Japan and all over the States. We usually took them to the Everglades National Park and Key West. The Everglades is a huge wetland, a slow moving river almost as wide as the Florida peninsula. It has alligators, turtles, and many species of birds. We walked by alligators a few times, but they ignored us. We usually got on a tram and enjoyed listening to a park ranger. We heard their stories countless times but learned something new each time. The major attraction of driving to Key West was the beautiful scenery on both sides of the Keys especially the Seven Mile Bridge near Marathon.

Miami was an ideal place to play tennis. Jim Hodgeman, whom we befriended at Serendipity and Ole Boys Bible class at Kendall UMC, introduced me to the group who played regularly at seven every Saturday morning throughout the year at King's Court, owned by a Baptist Church. We usually played doubles with whoever showed up. I played whenever I was in town; it hardly ever rained out. Jim was ten years older than I was but played evenly with me.

Jim and his wife, Barbara, had an annual potluck dinner for the Ole Boys Bible class and their spouses; after the dinner we always sang hymns from their old hymnal books. They had a summerhouse in Ketchikan, Alaska. They spent every summer there to escape the heat of Miami.

One time we visited their house in Ketchikan with Kei and the Hata family from Japan when we went to see Kei at Prince George. Kei was a graduate student at the University of North British Columbia at Prince George. Both the Hatas were friends of Shigeko from childhood. On the way we watched a bear catch a salmon in a stream.

Hodgeman's house was on the top of a hill near the port. The first morning we were surprised to see a huge cruise ship anchored at the port; its top-level cabins were the same height as the living room. It looked like a huge building and surprised us by coming up by the house suddenly overnight.

Jim took us out on his boat to fish for salmon. There were five of us, and we each caught a salmon within ninety minutes. Jim was impressed and told others back in Miami that we were very good. In reality it was Jim who knew where to go to catch fish. We merely threw in the lines. He threw away caviar as he cleaned the fish, and we were shocked. We told him that he is throwing away the best part of the fish. After that he brought us back caviars every year during our stay in Miami.

We enjoyed the house and the Florida weather until our children wanted us to move closer to them; they lived on the West Coast. They started to say this after three incidents of calling 911within a year, 2007–2008, because of me. I fainted twice, once due to dehydration and another due to staying in the Jacuzzi too long. The third incident happened when I slipped and fell in my study and cut my forehead. It bled profusely and scared Shigeko. All of these could have been averted by being more cautious. However, if something were to ever happen to me, we should be near one of our children.

We decided to move to Seattle to be near our son. This was Shigeko's choice because fish tastes better in Seattle than in California, where our two daughters were living. We sold the house and left in August of 2009; it took us about a year to pack. It was in the midst of a recession, but our realtor, Betty Brandon, was a member of the Serendipity class at our church; we'd bought the house from her. She was very conscientious and knew the market. We learned from her what price to ask and which buyer to choose. The price of the house decreased about 25 percent from the maximum, but we reasoned that the house in the Seattle area was also depressed by the equivalent amount.

PART V:

A PROGRESSIVE CHRISTIAN

CHAPTER 23:
EVOLVING AS A CHRISTIAN

I was not aware that I was baptized at St. Peter's Episcopal Church in Seattle soon after I was born. My mother was a Christian but did not teach me anything about Christianity. The only organized religion I noticed in Manchuria was Shinto. Its little shrine existed at a corner of the schoolyard of at least one school I attended, but I do not remember which school.

As soon as we got back to the States in January of 1948, my siblings and I started to go to the Japanese Methodist Church in Spokane, obeying Grandmother's wish, and each of us joined a Sunday school class. I did not have any interest in the Bible or sermons. However, I do remember Rev. Toyohiko Kagawa's visit. He was a well-known Japanese Christian among Americans of my grandparents' generation. He demonstrated with common laborers for their rights against the government prior to World War II. He mentioned Grand Coulee Dam in his sermon, but I do not remember in what context.

I got into the habit of going to church even after leaving Spokane. I went to churches of different denominations, even a Buddhist church, while attending the University of Washington, but usually I attended a Methodist church. In Madison, Wisconsin, my first roommate, Bob Hansen, was a devout Lutheran. Subsequently, when I shared an apartment with three other guys, one, Hiroshi Yamazaki, was a Christian. I do not remember ever going to church with them, but I did go by myself and usually to the Methodist Church and Wesley Foundation adjacent to the University of Wisconsin campus. By then I'd started to listen to the sermons, but often I did not like what a preacher said. When he said Christ is the only way to communicate with God or anything about exclusiveness of Christianity, I got upset and did not go to church for a while. One time I still remember as being ridiculous was when one said that no matter how good a person is, if he does not believe in Christ, then he goes to hell. Even a criminal if he believes in Christ he would go to heaven. I remember one person at the Spokane church who frequently went to the front of the congregation to ask for forgiveness for drinking too much, but he kept on drinking. However, at least in the Methodist churches, preachers gradually stopped saying that Christ is the only way to salvation, and by the time I went to Oak Ridge, they started to say there are more ways to communicate with God. When one said Gandhi led a life of an exemplary Christian, I was amazed. He was a well-known Hindu who was admired for practicing nonviolence in fights for justice. He refused to become a Christian. Martin Luther King, Jr., a devout Christian leader, followed Gandhi as an example in his fight for civil rights and social justice.

I made a vow with Shigeko, who grew up in a Methodist family in Japan, that we would join a church as soon as we settled down. Almost the first thing we did after going to Oak Ridge was join First Methodist Church (FMC). I called Reverend Shimada of the Japanese Methodist church in Spokane for the transfer of the membership. He was my father substitute at the commencement at Central Valley High School, and we interacted occasionally. He told me I was never a member of the Spokane church, Highland Park MC, but was a member of the St. Peter Episcopal Church in Seattle. I was baptized at St. Peter Episcopal Church, a Japanese church in Seattle at birth but was not aware that I was a member of that church until I tried to join the FMC in Oak Ridge. Thus, I became a member of FMC by the transfer of membership from the Episcopal Church. Methodist Church subsequently merged with United Brethren and FMC became the First United Methodist Church (FUMC).

Initially, I was a passive member going to the worship service on Sunday mornings accompanying Shigeko. She was a devout Christian with an associate degree in kindergarten education from Seiwa Junior College for Women, a Christian school established in about 1880 as Lambuth College for women by Mary Lambuth. She was the wife of Rev. James William Lambuth, a well-known Methodist missionary from Tennessee to China and Japan.

About ten years later, I decided I would go to an adult Sunday school class to learn about the Bible. I perceived Christianity as the basis of American culture and ethics, and I would learn about American culture and society by joining an adult Sunday school and interacting with its members. We joined the Upper Room Bible Class, a small class consisting of traditional fundamental Christians as well as more freethinking progressive Christians trying to find newer interpretations of the Bible more applicable to present society. It was an ideal class for me, and we went to the class almost every Sunday the rest of the time we were in Oak Ridge.

I did not learn traditional interpretations of the Bible while growing up. I studied the Bible for the first time while attending the Upper Room. We freely exchanged our own interpretations and asked questions. My interpretations and questions tended to be unique and more consistent with science. One of the first statements I made was that I did not believe angels exist. Traditional members of the group were upset. In similar manner I doubted miracles, but I learned to speak out only when I felt it was essential for me to do so and then with minimal disturbance. I enjoyed socializing with the members of the group and learned traditional views of the Christians of my generation. I enjoyed discussions on social, ethical, and cultural issues. Subsequently, when we moved to other cities, we searched for a Methodist church with an adult discussion group.

The most liberal member of the Upper Room was Mrs. Betty Oakberg. I still interact with her via e-mail, exchanging our views on issues in Christianity and society. She was a grade school teacher for two of our children. Our son had problems in reading, especially vocabulary, in the lower grade school years, and Mrs. Oakberg was one of the two teachers I discussed in Chapter 16-5. She is over ninety as of this writing, but her mind is still sharp.

I was asked to serve on commissions on missions, social concerns and church councils several terms over the years. I learned in the meetings of missions and social concerns that church members were more interested in aiding local needs than international needs, which I am interested in. I almost never volunteered but served when asked. Near the end of our stay in Oak Ridge, I served on the science and theology committee, which was the most interesting committee for me to serve on. The project it organized while I was serving on it is described in Chapter 23.

Council meetings at Oak Ridge indicated that the Methodist church is made up of people of diverse beliefs. The Methodist church finds unity in diversity, and we the members *are* the church. Jesus Christ exists within the heart and mind of each member, and God is revealed in each of the members through his teaching. Over the years I came to realize that on Easter we celebrate the resurrection of Jesus Christ who is alive in each of us. In the church I am currently attending, University Temple UMC, I realized that I am not the only one who does not accept God as "Father." We start our Lord 's Prayer, "Giver of life" instead of "Our Father."

CHAPTER 24:
GENETIC SCIENCE TASK FORCE OF UNITED METHODIST CHURCH

In 1988 the General Conference of United Methodist Church was authorized to form a task force to assess scientific developments in genetic engineering and its societal, ethical, and legal implications for all life-forms. The task force was formed the following year to discuss these issues with scientists, physicians, policy makers, attorneys, social workers, academics, theologians, ethicists, and persons affected by genetic disorders. I was appointed a member of the task force probably because of my experience in assessing biotechnology. We went to several places in two years. Most of the members were not scientists, but the host scientists took time to explain in simple terms what they were doing and the significance of their projects. The task force concluded that the church must be involved in examining appropriateness of the application of genetic science, but the scientists should be free to do basic research driven by curiosity that often leads to new knowledge.

The areas of special concerns raised were the patenting of life-forms and access to genetic technology, genetic medicine and therapy, screening and diagnosis of genetic diseases, prevention and therapy of these diseases, agricultural applications of genetic research, and environmental impacts. We recommended that guidelines should be established to determine appropriateness of a genetic research project and its applications, with input from the public. We reported our finding to several churches including First United Methodist Church of Oak Ridge. Our report in its entirety was inserted into the Methodist Resolution in 1992 (pp325 –337). It appeared also in Special Issue on Genetic Science in *Christian Social Action* (volume 4, January 1991).

First United Methodist Church of Oak Ridge has the Science and Theology Committee that regularly held symposia to promote interaction between scientific/technological and religious communities. I proposed to hold a symposium on the societal impact of human genetic engineering. We obtained a grant from the National Science Foundation to partially cover the cost of inviting speakers via the Philosophy Department of the University of Tennessee.

The symposium was held from October 18 to 19 in 1991. Experts in relevant fields were invited to talk: (1) Dr. Charles Cantor, molecular geneticist at Lawrence Berkeley National Laboratory, who held positions in the Human Genome Project of DOE-NIH, and of the International Human Genome Organization, talked on the benefit to society of research in molecular genetics and genetic engineering. (2) Rev. Kenneth Carder, senior minister at Church Street United Methodist Church in Knoxville, Tennessee, and the chairman of the Task Force of Genetic Engineering, talked on the findings of the task force dealing with social and ethical impacts of genetic engineering. (3) Dr. Glenn Graber, professor of philosophy at the University of Tennessee, talked on Bioethics of Human Genetic Engineering. (4) Bishop David Lawson of United Methodist Church in the Wisconsin Area, talked on Theological Issues and Dr. Roger Dworkin of the University of Indiana Law School talked on Legal Issues arising from Human Genetic Engineering. (5) Dr. Paul Billings of California Pacific Medical Center raised concerns about the Use and Misuse of Genetic Information in Society; (6) Ms. Marsha Saxton, Director of Project on Women and Disabilities, Boston, Massachusetts, raised concerns about Discrimination Against People Affected by Genetic Disorders; and (7) Dr. Paul Selby of the Biology Division, Oak Ridge National Laboratory, expressed concerns about the Deleterious Consequences of Accumulation of Defective Genes in the Human Gene Pool resulting from Improved Survival of the Carriers of Defective Genes.

As a researcher in basic life science, I agree with Rev. Ken Carder's remark that scientists should be free to gain knowledge, but we, the public, should be concerned with the consequence of the application of knowledge.

An unresolved question was whether to examine the genetic makeup of all individuals and reveal the defects to a person and his or her family when there is no cure for it. We made a videotape of the symposium for wider distribution of the proceeding of the symposium.

I lost my shyness and started to get involved in discussing issues relevant to sustainability of human civilization. Subsequently, Shigeko and I had moved to other places, and I sought a Methodist church with an adult Sunday school class where societal issues are actively discussed. This became more important to me than the worship service. Wherever I went I called myself a nontraditional Christian and expressed my views without regard to the beliefs of others. I think I was able to do this without antagonizing others because I was a minority; usually my wife and I were the only Asians, and I was the only scientist in the adult class we joined.

I think churches should make efforts to encourage rational dialogue between science and communities to sensitize the public on societal and ethical issues related to scientific knowledge and its application. I carried around a copy of the VHS tape of the Oak Ridge symposium to talk about the issues raised in genetic engineering to churches I subsequently attended.

Rev. Kenneth Carder became my mentor on Christianity. Subsequent to our serving on the task force, he served as the bishop of the Nashville and Mississippi Conferences and then became a professor of the practice of Christian ministry, Duke Divinity School. He retired from the professorship (2012), but I still seek his opinion occasionally.

CHAPTER 25:
INTEGRATION OF SCIENCE AND CHRISTIANITY/MY CHRISTIAN THEOLOGY

My main purpose of going to church almost every Sunday has been to integrate science into Christian theology. I spent my most meaningful times in adult Sunday school classes in churches I attended. I attended the Upper Room class at First UMC in Oak Ridge for about twenty years, and there I learned that each member had his or her own interpretation of the Bible and knew about the traditional interpretation. During that period we went through the Bible cover to cover at least twice and depended heavily on commentaries by William Barclay (1975). The Serendipity class at Kendall UMC in Miami had chances for any of its members to present lectures on any topics the speaker chose. I was an active member from 1995 to 2009. I presented many of my thoughts presented herein, as they were developed for the Serendipity class. We discussed societal, ethical, and theological issues without imposing Christian dogmas and miracles described in the Bible. As I aged, I socialized more and more within the Methodist community, and I am sensitized to world problems by interacting mainly with Methodists.

UMC had asked me to participate in a conference on science and theology in Nashville, Tennessee (October 18–20, 2002). The General Board of Discipleship (GBOD) was asked to submit a report on science and theology for the General Conference in 2004. The GBOD and General Board of Church and Society (GBCS) decided to invite some of the church members to find out what we thought about the subject. About fifty attended the conference. I was included along with some other members who had served on the genetic science task force. The three-day conference gave us an occasion to discuss openly some of theological issues of UMC. *The Book of Discipline* (2004, page 98), succinctly stated the conclusion of that conference—that science and theology are complementary rather than mutually incompatible, and I agree with the conclusion.

As progressive members of UMC said, we could follow the teaching of Jesus, ignoring the miracles mentioned in the Bible. The greatest miracle of Christianity is that millions of people all over the world still follow the teaching of a carpenter who preached only about three years and still worship him. Arts and cultures developed by Europeans and their offshoots in the New World have evolved from Christianity. The Bible stimulated intellectual thinking. I think modern science originated in Europe because the Bible had induced so many questions.

I was surprised to read recently in *Christianity: The Japanese Way* by Carlo Caldarola, (1979), that Uchimura Kanzo (1861–1930) criticized more than a century ago that Western Christianity as practiced in America is too materialistic and too denominational. After going back to Japan, he established the movement called *Mukyokai,* which means "nonchurch movement" (1901). It emphasized the teachings of Jesus Christ by noninstitutional small groups. I learned from Shigeko that Mukyokai exists today even in Seattle. They emphasize the importance of small groups, and therefore, they stayed small with no institutional organization. He also told listeners that he did not have to tell the Americans because they would come to realize this by themselves. Indeed, many have.

Around the same period as the conference in Nashville, Harry Switzer, while the choir director of the Kendall UMC, led a progressive Sunday school class, which I occasionally attended. He had introduced me to books by John Spong, Episcopal bishop (*Why Christianity Must Change or Die,* 1999) and Marcus Borg, professor of theology at Oregon State University (*The God We Never Knew: Beyond Dogmatic Religion to a More Authentic Contemporary Faith,* 1998). They are progressive theologians and advocated the removal of miracles from the Bible and the focus on God within each of us rather than a distant God. I agree with these and many other statements in their books. Subsequently, I also heard their lectures. Marcus Borg said in one of his speeches that he is a mainstream Christian. If so, my belief is no longer that of minority Christians; however, in reality I think the beliefs of Marcus Borg and I are still the minority.

Science and theological communities and the public should work together to sustain this civilization into the future. The resources of this planet are limited, and we are overpopulated. Could our science and technology keep up with overconsumption by our ever-increasing population? Christians should lead the public to less materialistic living and should respect all lives instead of being anthropocentric. This is consistent with the teachings of Buddhism and Shinto as followed by the Japanese prior to the post-World War II economic boom.

I believe God exists in a timeless, spaceless dimension, and we finite beings are incapable of understanding an infinite being, God. We perceive only manifestations of God seen in nature as those by Native Americans and Shintoists, and in Jesus by Christians. Christians have extrapolated from Jesus that his Father, God, has a human image; Michelangelo's painting on the ceiling of the Sistine Chapel in Vatican City represents this image of God.

Jesus is considered perfect based on biblical accounts of his life, but the Bible tells us only about a three-year period of his ministry. The Bible tells us also of the resurrected Christ who exists in each of us (Colossians 1:27) *today and into the future as long as there are his followers.* I call myself a nontraditional Christian because I try to follow Jesus's teachings and his actions, but I consider him a human.

More than fifty years ago while I was a postdoctoral fellow in Japan, I visited a Buddhist temple with a white gravel garden depicting a river of life flowing from its origin to the wide open ocean, Nirvana, and the monk explained to us that is life. The photo on the cover of this book is part of that garden. I did float with the current and fished out chance every time I needed one; each time it induced me to take an appropriate action that changed the course of my life. I would not know Nirvana prior to the end of this life.

In my mind, there is no discrepancy between scientific and Christian truth. Apparent discrepancy arose from the dogmatic views of fundamental Christians who believe that every word in the Bible is the word of God and scientists who think that knowledge obtained by scientific methods is the truth. Some physicists think that all truth can be expressed by mathematical equations. Scientific knowledge is based on information obtained by observations and experimentations on matter and energy and their interactions. These were verified many times by different methods accepted by the experts. Even after these verifications, scientists do not know their explanations are absolutely true.

Jews canonized the Old Testament near the end of the first century (85–90 AD). Gospels and letters in the New Testament were written from the middle of the first century to the middle of the second century, and the New Testament was first canonized in fourth century (Sundberg,

1971). I assume that for English-speaking fundamental Christians, the true version is the King James Version published in 1611. Christian theology, particularly Protestant theology, has been evolving, but the congregation generally has not kept up with the change. Since about 1600 our scientific knowledge has been increasing exponentially; our vocabulary increased, and the meaning of the words changed extensively. Therefore, we need to interpret the Bible in the present-day context rather than the interpretation of the past.

Our philosophy based on scientific knowledge has changed dramatically since the early twentieth century. Until Einstein's theory of relativity (1917), scientists generally thought that this universe was static and always in existence. When Einstein first derived his general theory of relativity, he did not believe his equation, which suggested that the universe was expanding, but twelve years later Hubble showed that the universe was indeed expanding. This raised a possibility that there was a beginning as stated in Genesis. Physicists proposed that our universe was created with the Big Bang 13.8 billion years ago. However, space-time prior to the Big Bang is infinitesimal, and how the energy was created that caused the Big Bang is incomprehensible.

In the early twentieth century another revolutionary theory was developed—quantum mechanics. Until that time scientists accepted Newton's theory, which showed that all physical observations could be determined exactly. However, in 1927 Heisenberg discovered that the position and the speed of a moving object of an atomic dimension could not be determined precisely (Uncertainty Principle). Quantum mechanics implies that scientific laws are not precise. If this theory is true, then it should be applicable to all matters at all dimensions.

Einstein tried to unify the general theory of relativity and quantum mechanics but failed. Currently, many theoretical physicists think that Super String/M theory is the unified theory (Greene, 2004). The fundamental unit of matter including energy is vibrating strings (one dimension) in Planck dimensions. The formation of two dimensional membranes by strings is called branes. Collisions of branes caused the Big Bang. There are infinite numbers of branes, and they are colliding frequently, creating infinite numbers of universes. The collision of three branes caused the Big Bang that created our universe. There are no ways to communicate between universes and no devices to get observable or experimental evidence for strings and branes. Super String/M theory is based on a mathematical equation, which is too complex to solve completely by theoretical physicists. They are just speculating based on approximate solutions, and their most accepted solution resulted in ten dimensions and time.

I am an experimental scientist and could not accept any scientific theories until proven by observations and/or experiments. These theoretical physicists have faith in mathematics and some manifestations of multiverse. Some think that all the mathematical solutions reveal truth, if not in this universe then somewhere in multiverse. If we cannot get any information about other universes, how could we test these theories?

Life evolved by the principle of the survival of the fittest to intelligent sentient beings that appreciate and admire this wonderful universe. The idea that everything was created by chance is too farfetched and unbelievable; it is as unbelievable as the idea of creation. I agree with Michael Behe, a biochemist, who wrote in *Darwin's Black Box* (1998) that some life processes at molecular levels are irreducibly complex. However, I do not agree with his conclusion that life is designed. It is too imperfect to be designed by omniscient, omnipotent God. I think at least one basic principle is missing, which may explain subjective experiences and spirituality. These may be as true as the objective observation revealed to modern scientists.

I accept the theory of evolution by survival of fittest because it is consistent with observations and experiments, but hypotheses on the origin of life from inorganic molecules are just conjectures based on circumstantial observations. We do not know how life originated. If it had occurred only once on this planet, then we would not be able to reproduce the event.

Science and religion have evolved and need to co-evolve into the future to understand this universe and the origin and meaning of our existence on this planet. The Bible is an excellent reference to understand how Jews and Christians understood our existence about two thousand years ago. We have free will and have gained tremendous amounts of knowledge by experiences, observations, and scientific experiments. We need to integrate this knowledge into theological/philosophical wisdom. Did our wisdom increase in parallel? No. Would we ever understand absolute truth and God? As a Buddhist monk once told me, we finite beings are incapable of understanding absolute truth, but we are still trying to understand it and God.

I am induced to believe in the existence of God by faith and my experiences, which I have described in this memoir. The God I believe is not the Trinity, as believed by traditional Christians. God does not have an image of man. Father and Son are idealized humans manifested to traditional Christians as God. I try to follow the teachings of Jesus Christ based on my interpretation of the Bible, and it is mostly consistent with current progressive theologians Marcus Borg and John Spong.

PART VI:

SUMMING UP THE LIVES OF THE FUJIMURAS AND MY ACTIVITIES

CHAPTER 26:
GRANDPARENTS AND PARENTS: LAST PHASE OF THEIR LIVES

Apparently, we came back to the States when my grandparents' business in Spokane, Ritz Café, was at the peak of its success. They bought their home in Opportunity, a suburb of Spokane, probably for their retirement. They brought us back from Japan in first-class cabins; came to San Francisco with Mrs. Alice Goto, wife of the pastor of the Spokane Japanese Methodist Church, to pick us up with a hired taxi driver in a Cadillac station wagon; and accommodated us in their little white house. It had a living room/dining room, a large kitchen, two bedrooms, and a full basement.

As I reflect back on that period, I do not know how seven of us slept in that house. The basement was too humid; most of its space was used for storage, and I used a large table for study. Grandparents lived in shifts with their twenty-four hour Ritz Café and their home. Grandfather worked during the day and slept at home at night, and Grandmother worked the graveyard shift and slept at home during the day. The big meal of the day was lunch when we did not go to school such as on weekends and during vacations. Grandmother talked about her family's tile business in Hofu. She was proud of the business; its tiles covered major buildings in Hofu such as Tenmangu, the Shinto shrine, and the middle school my father and I attended.

Grandfather had a heart attack prior to our arrival, but he recovered and was working all the time. He was either working or sleeping without any time for overt relaxation. His breakfast was a raw egg; he'd make a hole in one end and suck out its content while standing. I learned from him to fix things around the house, and I took over the care of the yard, chickens, and vegetable garden. The garden was planned and planted by a Japanese gardener. Grandfather and I irrigated it once a week during the night. The weather was dry, and we had to frequently water the lawn and garden.

Soon after our arrival, they acquired Mandarin Café, a Chinese restaurant (1948). Grandmother was proud of the restaurant, but it was not a profitable venture. The restaurant was located downtown, but customers had to climb up the stairs to get there. Grandfather kept the accounts of the business but never complained in our presence. I had to work as a waiter every New Year's Eve until about five the next morning. I did this until they got rid of the business; I remember working at least twice.

The family fortune went downward from that moment on. They sold their house in Opportunity in November of 1954; it was my junior year at the University of Washington. They leased the Great Northern Hotel at the corner of Stevens Street and Trent Avenue and bought its contents for seven thousand dollars. I do not think it was worth that much. It was at the edge of the skid row, near the Ritz Café. I worked at both places every vacation and got to know some winos who stayed at the hotel. One was a college graduate; when he was sober, he was critical of other winos. Many Native Americans from the Spokane Indian Reservation came to both places when they received monthly checks from the government and stayed around until they ran out of money, which was usually less than a week. Several had T-bone steaks for breakfast. At night several came to our hotel with spouses. Through the vent in the office, I could hear couples having sex.

In November of 1956, soon after I moved to Wisconsin, they had to move the Ritz Café from Trent Avenue to Main Street closer to the downtown area; the previous building was demolished. The new location was a nicer place but business was not as good.

Grandmother was the pillar of the Fujimura family. She was a liberated woman long before ordinary American women got liberated. She was a businesswoman first, and her chores as a housewife and mother were secondary. The ordinary Japanese woman's duty, even now, is to serve her husband and to bring up their children properly. Boys are expected to graduate from college, and girls are trained to be a proper wife by learning ikebana (flower arrangement), tea ceremony, and/or a musical instrument; Tamiko, our mother, learned to play piano. Grandmother never got along with her daughter because Grandmother's focus was on her business. Tamiko was sent to Japan, and her grandmother took care of her during her preschool years. While I was in Osaka during my postdoctoral period, I met Grandmother's step brother, who reminisced that he played with Tamiko during her stay.

Grandfather was working all the time. The only time he was relaxing was while he was asleep. He commuted by bus and often fell asleep and missed the bus stop at the front of his house. He went all the way to the end of the line near the Idaho border, and the bus driver had to wake him up on the return trip at the front of his house. Around Easter on April 17, 1960, he fell asleep after dinner and never woke up. He was seventy-nine.

After her husband's death, Grandmother—with the help of her adopted son, Tatsuo, my father—struggled for the existence of their hotels and restaurant. According to Jerry, my brother, they often had two hotels simultaneously around the skid row, a total of four all together; St. Regis was the best among them.

Great Falls Hotel was the only one they owned; the rest were on lease. They purchased it on September 1, 1973, and sold it on November 1, 1977. The proceeds were deposited to Father's estate, thinking that he would outlive Grandmother.

Father died unexpectedly in early 1980. As mentioned in chapter fifteen, I was very busy organizing the Gatlinburg symposium at the beginning of 1980. However, I felt an urge to see him and went to a life science conference in San Diego. On the way home, I planned to visit Mother in Seattle and Father in Spokane even though it was a roundabout way. The plane stopped at the Portland Airport on the way to Seattle. I made a courtesy call to Irene, who lived with her family in Portland, and I was disturbed to learn that Father was seriously ill. We decided all of us would visit Father in Spokane. In Seattle I met Mother, June, and Jerry, and Irene joined us. The last time we had gathered was at our grandfather's funeral in 1960. We went immediately to the hospital. Father was happy to see us, looked well, and wanted to have a drink and go out with us to eat. Our mother wet his lips with whiskey, which Jerry had retrieved from Father's room at the Randolph Hotel. His doctor told us that he had pneumonia but was recovering well and would be out of the hospital in a few days. We were relieved and stayed only about five minutes then left to go eat. That was the last time we saw him alive. That night, about 3:00 a.m., I was awoken by a choking sensation. I woke up Jerry, who was sharing a room with me at the Holiday Inn nearby and told him that there was poisonous gas in the room. Soon after that we got a phone call from the hospital that our father was dead. It was February 17, 1980. I was so glad I was able to see him prior to his death that at his funeral service two days later, I asked the preacher to read Psalms 150, which is a song in praise of God. I felt God had induced me to make the extra trip for me to see him even for a few minutes. I learned later that three-fourths of his lung was not functional; apparently, the doctor put us at ease by saying he was getting well. In retrospect a logical explanation for the timing of our father's death is that he relaxed so much seeing all of us that his body gave up the struggle to live. I have heard several similar cases where a patient died soon after seeing all of his or her family members.

Soon afterward I became the executor of the estate of Father to distribute the monthly proceeds from Great Falls Hotel to Grandmother and Mother, and I continued as an executor until the payments to the estate were paid up. At the time of Father's death, we were informed that my grandmother had to pay inheritance tax because Father was not Grandmother's son. I thought it was ridiculous and informed their lawyer that Father was the adopted son of Grandmother. My reasoning was accepted without questions, and we did not pay the tax.

Grandmother retired in 1979 and moved to Hifumien, a retirement home for the Japanese. Soon after Father's death, Grandmother could not take care of herself and moved to the Wisteria Retirement Home in Seattle. Mother and June went to help her. However, in about a year, Grandmother needed constant care and moved to the Restorative Care Center.

She had a roommate whose son-in-law and daughter, Mr. and Mrs. Bill Pugmire, came to visit often. Bill liked Grandmother so much that Bill came to see her even after she had moved to Keiro, the Japanese American nursing home, as soon as there was an opening (1987). At Keiro she had Japanese meals and entertainments. Bill and his wife visited her and took her frequently to her church, Blaine United Methodist Church, for the Japanese-language worship service and to Japanese movies even though they did not understand the language.

Grandmother passed away quietly in her sleep on July 2, 1988, at age ninety-four, satisfied with the successful life she led. She was the only one among my parents and grandparents who led her life the way she wanted and enjoyed her retirement.

After grandmother's death in 1988, the proceeds from Father's estate were distributed to Mother and to some of her grandchildren to assist in the cost of their college educations. The payments from the hotel were completed in 1997, and my job as the executor was finished. The monthly payments were small but were of benefit to them.

Mother's life was tragic. After coming back to the States, she worked for about five years as a waitress at the Ritz Café, but soon after I left for the university, she moved to Seattle with my two sisters and brother. She worked at several places but usually as a waitress in a restaurant similar to the Ritz Café. Apparently, she felt most at ease in such a restaurant. They had a difficult time making a living, even with the help of my siblings. Mother was bilingual and spoke both English and Japanese without an accent, better than her children. She could have easily qualified to work at a trading company or as an interpreter. However, she did not have the social etiquette or self-confidence to interact with people as equals.

When I went to Japan as a fellow of the Japan Society for the Promotion of Sciences with my wife in 1981, we had Mother over to our place in Oak Ridge to look after our kids. Shigeko introduced Mother to her friends, hoping her friends would come and keep her company. Friends did come, but Mother acted as if they were not welcome. Shigeko was perturbed when she learned about Mother's behavior from these friends. Mother's life was self-centered, watching soap operas on TV and going to Japanese movies when she had time. Her life was quite different from our social life in Oak Ridge.

In contrast, Shigeko's mother, Tomi, was very sociable. Our daughter Tomi was named after her. She came from Japan three times. She did not speak any English, but she knew how to socialize with guests without talking. Her social life in Japan was centered on her church and helping her friends and relatives. She was an excellent hostess and was well liked. She exchanged Christmas cards with several Oak Ridge friends until her death. Shigeko is like her mother and felt at ease in Christian communities. They are typical Methodists; they centered their lives on service.

After leaving Seattle for the University of Wisconsin and subsequent family life in Oak Ridge, I was busy with my life and visited mother only occasionally. Our children interacted with her only a few times. Perhaps because of this, she did not feel at ease with them and did not receive them with open arms. She gave us the impression that they were imposing on her during the few times they visited her. However, she did send presents to her grandchildren on Christmas and Easter. Tomi remembers best the baskets full of candies she and her siblings received each Easter, particularly a huge chocolate egg she received one Easter. Nevertheless, by the time her youngest grandson, Jonathan Genki, Jerry's son, was born, she was retired, relaxed, and enjoyed playing with him.

I talked with my mother over the phone frequently. The only topic I remember was complaints about her mother. I learned in one of these conversations that she did not want to come back to the States in 1948. She was disappointed that her husband gladly sent her back with their children to the States. She said this action showed her that he did not love her and gave it as the reason she divorced him within a few years after coming back to her parents in Spokane.

One time when I called, I distinctly smelled the donuts she used to make and mentioned it to her. Both of us were surprised because she was actually making donuts. Perhaps the molecules responsible for the odor were transmitted over the phone line, and my sensors in my nose were sensitized to it from the past (quantum entanglement?).

Mother may not have intended to sacrifice her happiness, but because of her marriage, we four children have had wonderful lives experiencing societies of both countries. I appreciate even the experiences in Manchuria. I am thankful to my grandparents and parents for providing me security in the turbulent period while growing up and then setting me free to develop my potential.

On August 1, 1998, we had our fiftieth anniversary reunion after starting our new lives as born-again Americans in Opportunity, Washington. The week prior to that reunion, Dan and we stayed at our time-share resort at Leavenworth, Washington, and invited anyone who would come to visit us; our two daughters lived out of town and did not come and showed up only for the weekend reunion. We, especially Shigeko, liked the Bavarian village atmosphere of the town. June and Roy came with us and stayed for a couple of nights. Then Frank, Irene, Jerry, Mari, and Genki came and stayed overnight. We went to see the *Sound of Music* at the outdoor theater.

Back in Seattle by the weekend, we had our family reunion dinner at the Asian Wok in Bellevue. All twenty-five descendants of Mother made it to the reunion—four children and their spouses; nine grandchildren, four of them with spouses; and four great grandchildren. We also had three of Roy's children and one of their friends. The next day we went to June and Roy's home for lunch. We all had a wonderful fiftieth reunion; we were happy and thankful to our mother for letting her children have successful lives blessed with wonderful families.

By the time we had the reunion, Mother had dementia, but she was aware of the occasion. However, soon after that her condition got worse, and she was moved to Keiro Nursing Home as soon as there was an opening, but she was not aware of the Japanese food and entertainments there, which she would have enjoyed. She died on September 13, 1998. I was holding Mother's hand until it got cold. Mother was the only one I was at the deathbed of my parents and grandparents.

In retrospect the lives of our parents and grandparents were a constant struggle. They suffered through a turbulent period of the Japan-US relationship. Our grandparents lost their business and properties in the States when they were forced to move to Minidoka soon after Pearl Harbor; they lost their farm in Japan by MacArthur's land reform, which took away land from absent landowners. Our grandfather worked until he died; the only time he was able to relax was during the time he lived in the concentration camp in Minidoka. Our grandmother lived throughout her life the way she wanted, no matter what it was like in the community they lived. I learned from Grandfather how to do minor repairs around the house and to keep busy doing something all the time. I learned from Grandmother to live the way I want by adjusting to the community in which we lived.

Our parents did not live much of their lives the way they wanted. Our father was a mystery to me. He went through two universities—received a law degree at Kansai University and a bachelor degree in political science at the University of Washington. I do not see the impact of his education in his life or writings. Perhaps the best time he had was when he was away from us, teaching high school students in Shizuoka. According to letters from his students and my cousins in Shizuoka, he was a popular teacher. He taught English and sociology. Perhaps his teaching in sociology was influenced by what he learned at the University of Washington. Our mother's life was spent under the influence of her mother; she was unhappy most of her life. She lived only a short time with her husband, and I never saw them socialize together. The only person I have seen her going out with was an accountant of my grandparents' business; they were together frequently during my high school days. I learned from our mother not to be dominated by others as she was, but to live according to my wish. I was an introvert and shy but learned to float down my path of life hooking opportunities as they came. I landed one every time I needed one.

CHAPTER 27:
OUR CHILDREN: EACH IN HIS/HER OWN CHOSEN CAREER

Shigeko is the ideal wife for me. She is the best wife I believe I could possibly have had, an excellent mother to our children, and an excellent host to our guests. She was brought up properly as a descendant of a samurai family. I am indebted to the Hasegawa sisters for inducing Shigeko's parents to approve me as her spouse. Subsequently, I found out that Shigeko was the favorite child of her mother. Although her mother never mentioned it, she must have missed Shigeko very much. When we got married, I wished Shigeko would become just like her mother and would bring up our children surrounded by her love. My wish was realized and our children grew up without any serious problems.

Dan and Tomi graduated from Oak Ridge High School the same year, 1982; Kei graduated in 1987 (Photo 27-1).

Photo 27-1: Left to right, graduation pictures of Dan, Tomi, and Kei

I was satisfied that I stayed in one place long enough for all of them to start and graduate from the same school system. Kei did make a detour to attend the American School in Japan during her junior year in high school while I was on a special assignment at the American Embassy in Tokyo. I went to six different schools prior to graduating from my high school and had to convert my primary language from Japanese to English, entirely different languages. I had never stayed in one place more than five years prior to Oak Ridge.

We let our children find their own professions. Each of them took a long time to find the profession they liked, but persisted. Tomi got to her profession systematically, more surefooted; Dan and Kei went through more changes in their pathways, but all have found their occupations and are happily married. We financially supported room and board for their undergraduate university studies—in the case of Dan, until he enlisted in the air force. The rest was their own. We are impressed and proud of their persistence and accomplishments.

27-1: Dan

Immediately after high school graduation, Dan followed two of his classmates to Tennessee Technical University in Cookeville, Tennessee. After the first year, he joined a group of his former Oak Ridge classmates and went to California to sell cookbooks "The Illustrated Encyclopedia of American Cooking, 1983. He took the old Toyota, which we had inherited from my father, for the venture. He charged all the gas expenses to me during the venture but had just enough for his living expenses. We have a copy of the cookbook and still use it occasionally.

When he restarted school, I found out he was on probation for bad grades. He should have switched to Roane State Community College but persisted.

When Shigeko, Kei, and I went to Japan on my special assignment, we rented our home to Tanaka Mitsuo and his wife and daughter. Dr. Tanaka was a visiting scientist on nuclear reactor safety, and they remained our close friends.

During our absence Dan came home on vacations and stayed in the basement, which had the master bedroom and family room. The house was on a slope and that side of the basement was above the ground level. During the Christmas holidays, he came to visit us in Tokyo and enjoyed New Year's Day events.

After we came back to Oak Ridge, he transferred to Roane State Community College in Oak Ridge, and soon thereafter he joined the air force (1988), which he had wanted to do from the time he got out of high school. His eyesight was not good enough to be a pilot, so he was assigned to a communication unit.

During the time he served, he moved from California to Korea to Japan to England and back to Nebraska. While at Offutt Air Force Base in Nebraska, he received his associate degree from the Community College of the Air Force and continued to study on computer information systems at Bellevue University located near the base.

Dan got out of the service in February of 1998 and received a bachelor of science at Bellevue University. We went to his graduation and were impressed by the talk by Tom Osborn, former coach of the University of Nebraska football. Dan worked at Anderson Consulting in Kansas City for a couple of years.

He settled down in Seattle in June of 2000 and started to work on contracts to test computer software. He married Nina Egasira at her Catholic Church (November 8, 2003). My cousins Yukio and Hideko, and Shigeko's sister, brother, and cousin Sadakazu's wife, came from Japan. Nina has seven brothers and sisters, and they were busy socializing with Nina's relatives. They did not interact much with my siblings. After a few years, they bought a house near Mill Creek, and that was the reason we eventually bought a house near them in 2009.

27-2: Tomi

The summer Tomi graduated from high school, she worked at Japan Pavilion at the 1982 World's Fair in

Knoxville. She interacted with many native Japanese and got interested in Japan.

She studied and obtained her associate degree in dental hygiene at East Tennessee State University in 1984 and then a bachelor of science in dental hygiene at the University of Washington in 1985.

In the summer of 1984, I drove with her to Seattle in our little Chevette, which was her graduation present. We camped along the way, but according to Tomi, I got a terrible cold and she drove most of the way.

In Seattle she had the chance to get to know her grandmother and great grandmother and Aunt June. She did not have much chance to get to know them while growing up, and she made the effort to interact with them as often as possible. By then her great grandmother was bedridden at a restorative care facility, and Tomi visited her as often as she could. She remembers one time she cooked her "somen," a Japanese noodle dish; she thought she made a huge excess, but she was amazed that Great Grandma finished eating all of it.

By the time Tomi received her degree, we were in Tokyo on my special assignment, and she joined us. Tomi got a dental hygiene position at a Japanese dentist's office, who catered to foreign clients. She was shocked that the Japanese did not take care of their teeth as much as average Americans, and their dentists did very sloppy jobs of cleaning and repairing teeth, except her dentist. *Recently (2011), I learned from TV that the Japanese dentists were going to China to treat the Chinese with modern techniques and are very popular there. They must have improved during the past twenty-five years.*

She attended courses at Sofia University in Tokyo, mainly to learn Japanese. Until that time the only Japanese she knew was colloquial language that she picked up from her mother. She joined a travel club at the school and traveled all around Japan. She was thankful to her mother for instructing her in detail wherever she went. As she came to understand Japanese, she learned about her mother better and respected her more.

After returning to Tennessee, she wanted to get into international business and took introductory courses in political science and business at the University of Tennessee. She went on to Thunderbird School of Global Management in Arizona, well known for combining cultures and languages in business. It is considered the number one school on international business. Tomi wanted to go back to Japan and, therefore, focused her studies on Japan. She already learned to speak and write some Japanese and was able to jump right into learning business Japanese. She felt at home surrounded by foreign students; she did not have to explain her background and made some lasting friendship.

Tomi did an internship in Japan at Banyu Pharmaceuticals, Inc. a subsidiary of Merck Pharmaceuticals in the United States. Dr. Susumu Nishimura, my colleague at the National Cancer Center, had introduced her to the company. She learned that Japanese, in general, talk in round about ways, which I call helical ways—round and round, never getting to the point. The listeners have to deduce the take-home message. I noticed that the American government officials who visited Japan wanted a take-home message instantly and got upset dealing with the Japanese. Japanese society is hierarchical. The most superior man speaks, and the rest keep quiet; women generally do not get managerial positions.

Tomi graduated from Thunderbird in 1991 and worked in Japan for three years, mainly at Banyu Phamaceuticals. By the end of that period, she decided she wanted to go back to America; she realized she is an American. I admire her for staying in Japan in the midst of the Japanese that long. When I would live in Japan for a year, I would feel like getting sick, living among crowds of people; I have never lived there for more than fifteen months continuously.

My assignment at the embassy in Tokyo was for fourteen months. I declined an offer to stay longer in a similar position. Shigeko loves a large city and felt like she was in heaven living in the center of Tokyo in an American style apartment. Later, when she found out that I could have stayed longer, she was upset.

By the time Tomi came back to the States, Shigeko and I had moved to Bethesda, Maryland (1992). I was doing research on HIV-associated dementia at a FDA laboratory (chapter 19). She worked at a spice company in Baltimore where she met Jan Sysmans from Belgium. He came to visit Tomi in our townhouse and stayed overnight in the basement in my study room a few times.

In 1995 we moved to Miami (chapter 20). Tomi was looking for some jobs more relevant to her professional training. One day by chance, I looked at the Miami Herald classifieds and noticed an opening at Cordis, a medical device company. I sent the ad to Tomi; she came down for an interview and was hired. She moved in with us.

Soon, Jan and Tomi got married and had a big wedding in Antwerp, Belgium (October 5, 1996). We went there and stayed by a beach about ninety miles away at a time-share resort. We commuted for the social functions but stayed in Antwerp on the wedding night. They had the wedding reception at the company of Jan's father. Jan's father, Sis, was involved in labor relations and received two awards in Japan for it. We had twelve guests from Japan, which included Shigeko's classmates and their daughter, former Oak Ridgers and Shigeko's sister and cousin Sadakazu's wife. We had Irene from Portland and Shigeko's classmate and her spouse from Chicago. Tomi had some of her classmates from Thunderbird. It was a great party; we danced until late at night. Jan was willing to move to wherever there was a job for Tomi. They stayed in Miami for about three years and had our first grandchild, Carolyne, in 1998. They soon moved to Silicon Valley, California, where Tomi found a better job to market medical devices.

They bought a house in Sunnyvale, and soon had another child, Eryk. As they grew older, I enjoyed them more with minimal responsibility. A memorable occasion was the trip we made to the Smoky Mountain National Park in the spring of 2011; the mountains were covered with fresh green leaves and with dogwood flowers blooming here and there. We took a hike with

Carolyne and Eryk to Abrams Falls from Cades Cove and took a few steps onto the Appalachian Trail near Newfound Gap. We reminisced that these were the two places we visited most often with their mother, uncle, and aunt while they were growing up.

27-3: Kei

After graduating from Oak Ridge High school in 1987, Kei went to American University in Washington, DC for one year to study foreign relations, but she lost interest in it and went to the University of Wisconsin-Madison for three years and received her Bachelor of Science in sociology in 1991, the same year Tomi received her Master of Science at Thunderbird. Shigeko and I with Dan drove first to the graduation of Kei in Madison, and then we stopped over at Mesa Verde National Park in Colorado where we saw village remains of ancient cliff dwellers and climbed into one of them. We drove through Monument Valley, stopped at the south side of the Grand Canyon, and went to Phoenix, Arizona, to attend Tomi's graduation from Thunderbird. Tomi made us pull a trailer full of her stuff back to Oak Ridge. We drove through Petrified Forest National Park and marveled at the huge petrified tree stems.

Kei went to Seattle and worked for a while but realized there were no good jobs as a sociologist and went to Oregon State to study ecology, 1996–1999. After getting her Master of Science, she went to the University of Northern British Columbia at Prince George for her PhD. Her thesis project was to study the effect of global warming on fungal communities as glaciers melted in arctic ecosystems. She collected specimens at Alexandra Fjord on Ellesmere Island in Nunavut, Canada, northwest of Greenland.

About one year prior to her PhD, we went on a cruise to Glacier Bay National Park as her graduation present (2004). Our cruise ship was small, only nineteen people. Therefore, we were able to go upstream where big cruise ships could not go. We were divided into three groups; Shigeko and I were the only people in our group because there were no other old people like us. We were provided with a kayak and taught how to use it. It was the first time Shigeko and I were on a kayak, and it was a stable kayak made for novices like us. There were three naturalists on our cruise. They took turns rotating among the three groups; therefore, each day we had a different naturalist all by ourselves. We explored different areas each day for five days. The ship moved around the bay during the night to a new location. We hiked on some islands. We used bear trails and kept on shouting "Hi bear" to scare away any bears that might have be around.

Anyone who has not been to Glacier Bay should do so prior to the disappearance of glaciers; we saw huge chunks of ice falling into the sea often. They were magnificently beautiful sights. We saw whales, killer whales, seals, and other marine life swimming around the sea. We also saw many eagles flying over us and bears and goats on land.

Kei received her PhD in August of 2005, came down to Seattle, looked for a job in ecology, and worked as a postdoctoral fellow, but she found nothing she liked.

She changed over to do medical research. Through a connection she found a postdoctoral position at the University of California Medical School at San Francisco to do research on pathological microorganisms in human guts (June 2008).

Since her graduate-school days, Kei had been going steady with Ed Kraay, who lived in Seattle. One day Ed called me up and asked me in Japanese for permission to get married to Kei. I was surprised that Ed spoke in Japanese. However, we were expecting them to get married, and I promptly gave my permission. They had the wedding and the reception on Lopez Island in the northern part of Puget Sound on September 13, 2008. I'd never heard of the island until they decided it would be the wedding site. We learned that it was Kei's favorite hiking place. It was a remote place accessed only by a ferry. However, Kei's friends and relatives came from far and wide—Wisconsin, Washington, DC, Oregon, and British Columbia; Shigeko's sister, cousin's spouse, and classmates from Japan; and Jan Sysmans parents from Belgium. Shigeko and I had to pick up our guests from Japan at the Vancouver International Airport in British Columbia and send them off from there afterward. Soon after, we helped Kei and Ed pack and move to San Francisco. Ed decided to move to San Francisco and find a job there.

They have settled down in San Francisco. In October of 2010, they had a son, Simon Kousuke Robert. Kei induced us to be connected via Skype; we were not aware such a device existed until Kei got it for us. We see our grandson at least once a week via Skype and feel as if we are watching him grow up near us.

Kei became a research associate in 2011. Research on pathological microorganisms in human guts is an exciting field; I notice articles on the subject frequently.

27-4: Grandpa and Grandma

In the summer of 2011, my cousins from Tokyo, Yukio and Hideko, came for a visit, and we drove to Yellowstone National Park. We had a wonderful trip; it was a memorable trip for my cousins. We drove through Spokane to show where Ritz Café used to be and to Opportunity to show them where I lived in my high school days (chapter 10). Then on the return trip, we went to Camp Minidoka where my grandparents were interned during the war. Therefore, both Yukio and Hideko have been to every place my grandparents, their uncle, and I lived in the States, except Wisconsin. When we returned from Yellowstone, most of our relatives gathered and had a picnic. Thirty-one people from my siblings to our children and grandchildren showed up, many from out of state; this impressed our cousins. On that occasion our daughters, their spouses, and our grandchildren came from California; so we had our family pictures taken by a professional photographer (photo 27-2).

Photo 27-2: Grandparents surrounded by our three grand-children, three children, and their spouses

All our grand-children are mixed blood. In 2012 non-whites, if Hispanics are included, became the majority among the American citizens. Prior to Barack Obama being elected as the president of the United States, I did not dream that a person mixed with non-Caucasian blood would be elected in my lifetime. I am proud of the younger generations; a large majority of them voted for him, and we reelected him in 2012. The younger generation may have become blind to ethnicity when electing the president and chose the best qualified among the candidates from both parties. This means one of our grand-children may become the president of the United States. Would we ever become blind to a candidate's religious beliefs?

Photo 27-3: Our fiftieth anniversary dinner

We had our fifti-eth wedding anni-versary on Dec. 1, 2012. We gathered on the Christmas holidays to cer-ebrate that occasion at Tomi's house in Sunnyvale, Califor-nia. (Photo 27-3)

CHAPTER 28:
ULTIMATE PERIOD OF MY SCIENTIFIC ACTIVITIES

28-1: Veterans Affairs Puget Sound Health Care System in Seattle

When we moved to Seattle to be near our son, I wanted to continue doing experiments in a laboratory for as long as possible. One day I noticed an advertisement on the Alzheimer Research Forum by Dr. Suzanne Craft for an associate director in neurodegenerative diseases at the Geriatric Research Education and Clinical Center (GRECC), Veterans Affairs Medical Center (VAMC), on Puget Sound in Seattle. I decided to inquire, stating that I am not responding to the position in the advertisement for I am retired, but I would like to have a position as a volunteer. I wrote that I have been doing research on expression of genes essential for

memory, mitochondrial and synaptic functions in Alzheimer's disease cases (letter dated July 24, 2008). I
received a prompt response referring me to Dr. David
Cook of the same department. We met while Shigeko
and I visited Seattle for the wedding of Michael Nishi-
moto, our nephew, which was on April 4, 2009. I promised I would work for him as soon as we moved to the
Seattle area.

We moved at the end of August of 2009. Dan and his
wife lived near the Mill Creek shopping center north
of Seattle, and we bought a house in October, less than
four miles away, east off Seattle Hill Road, in a wooded,
quiet residential area. The house was almost new, built
in 2002, and met our criteria of a small yard, a one-story
house, and a location near a bus stop. I joined the Cook's
laboratory at GRECC, VAMC, in October. I commuted
by a bus. I enjoyed the bus ride reading, listening to an
audio book or favorite radio or TV program on my iPod,
or sleeping.

The focus of the Cook's laboratory is cellular and
molecular biology relevant to Alzheimer's disease. I
was assigned to analyze by real-time polymerase chain
reaction (PCR) the expression of relevant genes in Alzheimer's disease cases and its mouse models. The pace
of the laboratory was slow coordinating the findings with
other laboratories. I was clearly from a different generation. I liked to do exploratory experiments continuously
to keep myself busy, and if I observed something that
arose my curiosity, I confirmed my findings by extensive experiments. Current research laboratories, not just

Cook's laboratory, would minimize failed experiments by depending on techniques well-developed by others and tried to confirm the findings of others. The administration at VAMC has too much power and makes us take meaningless courses annually. Within a year we finished the project I was participating in, and when I had to take these irreverent courses, I gave up the privilege of doing experiments and became a consultant (September 2011). I taught a postdoctoral fellow in the laboratory how to do real time PCR and gave him typed out, detailed protocols for the procedures. More than two years later, Cook's laboratory started to have group meetings regularly; I attend them as often as I could to keep up on research of the group.

28-2: University of Washington

Meanwhile, I reconnected with Professor Larry Loeb at the Pathology Department at the University of Washington School of Medicine. My former PhD student, Shishir Das, came to Larry Loeb's laboratory as a postdoctoral fellow around 1984 (chapter 16). Larry's group has been studying mutagenesis by focusing on fidelity of DNA replication from that period, and when I visited Larry Loeb, he had invited me to participate in his research group meetings, which often had guest speakers. I have been attending most of his group meeting ever since. It has updated my knowledge of DNA polymerases and DNA replication and repair.

I am an alumnus of the University of Washington and explored what I could do there. Unlike the University of Miami, I could go into any buildings I wanted. The facilities I have been using most are its libraries—Suzzallo & Allen, Odegaard, and East Asia. I can download any restricted scientific journals I want as long as the library subscribes to them. I am impressed by the collections at the East Asia Library. It has major Japanese magazines on politics, social issues, and arts—Bungei Shunjuu, Sekai, Seiron and many others. I can check out these magazines to keep up with current and past issues.

Within a year I checked out and read classic scientific books such as Charles Dawin's *Origin of Species*, and Erwin Schrodinger's *What is Life*. I read books by authors in my own field of research such as Arthur Kornberg's *Love of Enzymes* and Harrison Echols's *Operators and Promoters: The story of Molecular Biology and its Creators*. I shared the same laboratory with Hatch Echols in the Department of Biochemistry at the University of Wisconsin during the time I was with Kaesberg after coming back from Japan in1963. I was surprised to find and read such old Japanese books as *Mirror for Americans: Japan* by Helen Mears (1948); *Christianity: The Japanese Way* by Carlo Caldarola (1979); *The Autobiography of Ozaki Yukio, 1858–1954* (English translation 2001); *Bushido, The soul of Japan* (1905), and *The Japanese Nation* (1912) by Nitobe Inazo. I read these books within the first two years I was here and cited some of these books at appropriate places in this writing. I realized that the university libraries could keep me intellectually stimulated for many years to come. However, I am not sure my eyesight would keep up with my desire to read. As of this writing, I cannot read much longer than twenty minutes before I can no longer focus on printed matter. I depend more and more on audio books via iPod.

I attended seminars at the University of Washington, especially those offered for the public. During 2010 the first year I was here, I thought the series on the alternate source of energy at Kane Hall and the Mini-Med Series at the medical school were excellent. They dealt with current problems and possible solutions. Subsequently, I have been attending public lectures whenever possible.

28-3: Life Science in the Twenty-First Century

The greatest unsolved problem in molecular biology is the relationship between the mind and the brain. The mind is in the brain. Do we know what it is? When we understand the mechanisms of cognition and consciousness, would we understand the mind? When we consciously express what we have in our mind, we call it the will. When we understand the will, would we understand the mind? Does reflexive action come from the mind? It is much quicker than conscious action, and the mind has to stay alert to control it. Memory is retrieved from the brain. On March 1, 2013, I heard a lecture by Daniel J. Siegel, a neuropsychologist at Harvard. He gave an excellent summary of the relationship between the brain, body, and mind. I got from his talk that the mind integrates memory, which resides on the right side of the brain, and senses received from the body and rationalizes the information obtained. The mind is in the prefrontal lobe and controls the response of the lower brain.

The mind is not fully developed in children, and the right brain tends to control our actions, which are irrational.

Serious researches are being done to understand consciousness. The conferences on science of consciousness are held on a regular interval at the University of Arizona. I attended two of them—Toward a Science of Consciousness (April 10–15, 2000) and Quantum Mind (March 15–19, 2003). Will we elucidate the mechanism of consciousness within this century? I was amazed to listen to an audiobook recently by a philosopher who said it is unlikely that scientists would ever deal with the mechanisms of consciousness.

I noticed from the 2000 conference that nobody dealt with molecular biology of consciousness, and I presented a poster on the subject at the 2003 conference. I concluded in the poster that combined efforts in molecular genetics, biochemistry, pharmacology, and other disciplines are needed to elucidate the mechanisms of consciousness. I was surprised to be informed that Google had a photo of me presenting the poster.

28-4: Concerns for the Future of our Civilization

Planet Earth is overpopulated with humans, and we do not have any strategy to reduce the population. Louise Leakey in her lecture (February 4, 2010) at the University of Washington showed a human population growth curve and said that we are near the saturation point. The habitats of wildlife need to be preserved to maintain biodiversity, but humans are destroying them. She is a granddaughter of Luis Leakey, the discoverer of the evidence for the human origin in Africa. I heard him speak about human fossils in Africa at the Sigma XI lecture at the University of Wisconsin-Madison in 1959. Louise Leakey observed with horror that the bulging human population is displacing the wildlife in Africa, and her husband is working for the preservation of biodiversity.

China limited Hans, the major ethnic group, to one child per family, but it caused the imbalance in sex ratio, and this policy could not be sustained. Probably the education of the female is the best solution to suppress the population growth as indicated by the growth rate approaching zero in the developed countries. Among the developing countries, there are those that discourage or prevent the education of females.

Up to present, science and technology enlarged the capacity of the planet for humans to live with sufficient amounts of food and materials, at least in the developed societies. However, our energy consumption cannot be sustained with petroleum as the major source; it causes pollution and global warming. During 2010 I listened to lectures on alternate sources of energy at the University of Washington. When it was over, I was depressed because there is none that could displace petroleum. Then I heard the lecture on the development of the new, efficient material graphene to capture solar energy. The university has a new department with a new building to develop this technology. This gave me confidence that human ingenuity would develop new technologies to make us energy sufficient with clean energy.

The planet cannot accommodate the standard of living of the people of China and India to attain that of middle class America unless we develop renewable resources and minimize pollution. The profit-oriented capitalism that depends on consumer debt is unsustainable. Our economy should depend less on material consumption. We need other incentives to live. Michio Kaku, a theoretical physicist, suggested in his book, *Physics of the Future*, 2011, that "Intellectual Capitalism" is the solution. He noted that most of the scientists and engineers are satisfied with solving problems and satisfying their curiosities. If a large fraction of us practice these and other professions that strive to satisfy our curiosity instead of our material comfort, we would be satisfied with sustainable levels of material wealth. I am an example of one who practiced what he proposed and believe that we should be satisfied with a curiosity-driven life.

The frontier of science and technology is endless as long as we do not destroy ourselves and can control the population of humans and keep the consumption to a sustainable level. According to another book by Michio Kaku (2008), almost everything mentioned in science fictions is possible, but some may take millions of years. According to Roger Penrose, another theoretical physicist, the possibility of life to originate and evolve to sentient beings is 1×10^{-127}. This means impossible, but we exist! I think the fundamental principle that would explain the origin of life is missing; random processes are not sufficient. Mechanisms of DNA recombination and replication errors explain the variations in gene pools.

Survival of the fittest explains the process of evolution. Humans have learned to control which organisms would survive and to alter them for the benefit of mankind. Are we wise enough to control all the processes on Planet Earth for the perpetuation of life on this planet? Are we strong enough to suppress emotional desires to sustain quality of life at optimum levels?

CHAPTER 29:
ULTIMATE PERIOD OF MY CHRISTIAN ACTIVITIES

29-1: University Temple United Methodist Church (UTUMC)

When we moved to Seattle, we searched for the church most appropriate for our religious interests. Shigeko found that the Japanese Presbyterian Church has members of her age group who liked to listen to sermons in Japanese and had similar backgrounds in Japan. They call themselves "new Issei." They are Japanese immigrants after World War II. Shigeko belongs to that category. For me the English-speaking congregation of the church was too conservative. We had an interview with the primary pastor and the Japanese language pastor of that church. I told them what I believed. I said Jesus was a human, and they got upset and told me that I am welcomed only to socialize. I was glad they did not accept me to become a member.

I found progressive members at the University Temple United Methodist Church adjacent to the University of Washington most stimulating. During the Enrichment Hour each Sunday morning, the group listens to a speaker or watches a video on nondogmatic theology, social issues, and ethics followed by rational discussions. Also men gather every Saturday morning for breakfast to discuss current social, political, and theological issues. Our pastor, who joined the church after I came, is very socially active and organizes events under "Common Good Café" at least once a week during the evening. People from surrounding communities, mostly nonmembers of the church, gather and listen to invited speakers on various issues followed by discussions. I feel I found a church that satisfies my curiosity to learn as much as I could about human nature. I am planning to participate in these church activities as long as I am mentally and physically capable.

29-2: Emmaus Support Center for the Survivors of 3.11 at Ishinomaki, Japan

About a half-year after the East Japan Earthquake and Tsunami (March 11, 2011), I sent inquires to find out whether I could do volunteer work for restoration of the disaster area. I received a mail via United Methodist Volunteer in Mission (UMVIM) that Northeast Christian Church of Japan (Kyodan) was looking for a bilingual, bicultural person to work as a coordinator of foreign volunteers at Emmaus Support Center in Ishinomaki Miyagi Prefecture, a newly created position. United Methodist Commission on Relief (UMCOR) had donated a fund for the work of Emmaus Support Centers to Kyodan, which has the main center in Sendai, and that may have been the reason they looked for a Methodist. I accepted the position to act as a temporary staff member from the beginning of 2012 until the retired pastor could replace me in June. In actuality I was there from February 14 to June 7, and no one came from the States to replace me, but the position was replaced by a Kyodan member. There were usually three or four staff members besides me; most of the time, I was the only Christian. The volunteers came from all over Japan, from Okinawa to Hokkaido, and rotated with new volunteers every week and worked from Monday to Friday, mostly non-Christian young adults of college age. During my tenure two groups came from the United States—one from Cedar Park UMC in Texas and another from Sacramento Japanese UMC in California. The Texas group was high school students with a few adults as chaperons. The Sacramento group was Japanese Americans consisting of twenty to sixty year olds. One lone Iranian American came, introduced by her cousin, a missionary pastor who had come for a visit to Ishinomaki Support Center a few weeks earlier with a group consisting of members of UMVIM and UMCOR.

Until I went there, I was not aware that a tsunami was not a simple wave; a front of a raised body of seawater higher than the shore rushed in and flooded the whole lowland area and stayed there for a few days. In the Ishinomaki central city section, the tsunami came more than a mile inland and flooded the first floor of houses to about eight feet just below the ceiling, and salt water damaged everything that got submerged. I heard that fish were swimming around inside the houses. One of the major projects for the volunteers was to peel off drywalls and floors and remove the mud from underneath. Sliding doors made of papers or screens were replaced, and wooden pillars, partitions, and floors were varnished and waxed. Outdoor sidings made of metal sheets were repainted. We painted some in freezing weather, the first time I ever painted in such cold temperatures. As the temperature got warmer, we helped restore gardens by replacing salted soil and spreading manures, dug out roots of dead bushes, and pulled out weeds. We even shifted gravel from driveways to remove dirt. The residents were older people and would not be able to maintain these houses inside and out. They welcomed the interaction with young volunteers and served us refreshments and sometimes even hot lunch. The volunteers felt worthwhile coming and interacting with them; several came back many times, and the staff members were selected from such volunteers. I think support centers like Ishinomaki are needed permanently all over the country to carry out these chores and for young people to interact with these elders.

The goal of our work was to restore the community and to promote socializing among them. Kyodan had built a temporary community center at the area in Sendai

that was damaged extensively but restored by the volunteers. On one of the days during the Golden Week (April 29–May 5), the volunteers and local people gathered and had spe-

Photo 29: *At the front of Sasayashiki Community Center, Sendai*

cial entertainments including a local folk dance. Photo 29 shows four of the volunteers and Shigeko and me at the front of the community center. To promote social interactions, the staff invited performers to the Ishinomaki Support Center and temporary housings. They were glad to entertain the survivors voluntarily. At temporary housings, teatime gatherings were organized to make handcrafts. A center nearby the apartment we were staying had hired a businessman, who had lost his business office, to teach local residents computer skills. Shigeko joined in these activities and socialized with these survivors.

There were many houses with the first floor damaged; some had people living on the second floor, and others were vacant. It would take many more years for the communities to be restored and to thrive. People were smiling and friendly, coping with their conditions. When we went shopping in malls adjacent to the disaster area, there was an abundance of food and necessities and some luxury goods. Shoppers looked and dressed just like any other places as if they were not aware that adjacent to these places were many vacant lots and houses.

The Japanese like to relax at hot-spring resorts with gourmet dinners and breakfasts. There are many places like this nearby Ishinomaki and Sendai. Shigeko had joined me in April, and we went to some of these places on Saturday evenings and stayed overnight. We went to a couple on a cliff by the sea; these were damaged but were restored by the time we went there and doing business at full capacity. One was in Matsushima, the place included as one of the three most scenic spots in Japan. It was only about a thirty minute drive from our apartment, but we managed to go there only once. It is located in a bay with many islands. The tsunami was partially blocked by these islands, and the town was fully restored and thriving by the time we went there.

On the week of the spring break, we went to Ueno Museum in Tokyo to see the exhibit of Japanese art that came from the Boston Museum. One was a drawing of a huge dragon that has never been seen in public in Boston. Yukio drove us back from Tokyo to Ishinomaki, stopping over at two onsens along the way and a couple of spots known for beautiful cherry blossoms. Yukio was a graduate of Tohoku University in Sendai, and when we went up to Hiyoriyama Park located at the top of a hill, he was overcome with emotion and had tears in his eyes as he observed the vast, vacant land toward the sea about a couple of miles away. Formerly, the area was packed with houses, and now only a few vacant buildings remained; one was an abandoned hospital. Piles of debris and wrecked cars were visible along the shore.

After my work at Ishinomaki Support Center was finished, we spent an additional three weeks in Japan and stayed one week in Tokyo at Shigeko's cousin Hisako's house, who lived on the same lot with her brother Ichiro's family, and another week near Osaka with Shigeko's sister Noriko's family. Each day, we went out and was entertained by our friends and relatives in these areas. We spent almost a week at my cousin Hideko's newly remodeled house in Karuizawa. My cousin Yukio also joined us. Karuizawa is a resort town near Mount Aso in Nagano Prefecture; the town is well-known as a summer resort for high-society people.

As I finished writing this section, we observed the second anniversary of 3.11. NHK TV showed the scenes from Ishinomaki. The scene from Hiyoriyama has not changed from a year ago. The land between the park and sea was vacant. Houses with damaged first floors were also shown. According to a staff member at Emmaus Support Center, the owners of these houses are not known.

The most lasting damage caused by the Great Earthquake of East Japan is the radiation leaks from the nuclear power plants in Fukushima. For a long period after the war, nuclear power was considered the primary alternate source of energy that would eventually replace fossil fuels, but the safety problems, as revealed by the nuclear power plant accident in Fukushima on 3.11, suggest that it could never be a major source of energy. Japan depended on nuclear power for 30 percent of her needs. She switched back to fossil fuel, especially natural gas; this cannot be sustained. Her CO_2 emissions had remained constant recently, but now it is increasing. Her use of renewable energy for electricity has been only 2 percent of the total. In my opinion solar power should become the major source of energy, and Japan should take leadership in developing it.

POSTSCRIPT: IMPACT OF THE UNITED STATES OF AMERICA ON MODERN JAPAN (HISTORICAL FACTS AND DATES ARE BASED ON JAPAN CHRONIK, 1991)

The United States of America had direct influence on modernization of Japan, probably more than any other country. First was the forced opening of Japan by Commodore Perry and his black ships after more than 250 years of isolation. Next was the occupation of Japan by allied forces led by General Douglas MacArthur (September 2, 1945) and the birth of the democratic form of government.

CHAPTER 30:
JAPAN AWAKENING TO THE WORLD DOMINATED BY EURO-AMERICAN POWERS

Japan had been self-sufficient; they had lived in peace under Tokugawa Bakufu (feudal regime) from the time the Osaka castle was burned down and the heir to Hideyoshi committed suicide (1615) to the arrival of the black ships (1853). The peace lasted for 238 years, longer than the Pax Romana, which was for 207 years.

The Bakufu gradually enforced the isolation policies to prevent colonization of Japan. Tokugawa Bakufu had perceived that Christian missionaries had assisted in colonization of East Asia by the European powers, and therefore, persecuted Christians. The Japanese were prohibited from going out, and those living outside were prohibited from coming back to the country (1633). Only the people from the Netherlands, among the Europeans, were permitted into Japan and only at Nagasaki (1636). Merchants from the Netherlands had convinced the Bakufu that they would only trade and would not spread Christianity.

Through the news from Nagasaki, the Japanese were aware of the dominance of European and American powers over China and the humiliating semicolonial subjugation of China, the country they respected the most. Tokugawa Bakufu thought that they could avoid the Western dominance by maintaining isolationism. However, the visit of the black ships led by Commodore Perry shocked and convinced many, especially young samurais, that the Tokugawa Bakufu would not be able to keep the Americans and Europeans away.

Under the peaceful Tokugawa Bakufu, the samurai class did not have much to do as the warriors. They practiced *kendo* (swordsmanship) as the training to instill *Bushido* (Yamato Damashii, Japanese spirit), and studied *jukyo* (Confucianism integrated into Shinto). The emphasis was on wisdom rather than knowledge. Samurais contributed to the refinement of Japanese art and literature. Near the end of the Bakufu period, many samurais had time to venture into new things such as business and Western technologies. Even the farmers were literate; probably the literacy rate was the highest in the world.

Minamoto Yoritomo established Bakufu system of government around 1190, and the emperor stayed in the background. The most powerful samurai, usually the winner of a civil war, claimed himself to be on the side of the emperor. Tokugawa Ieyasu established the last ba-kufu, which ruled for 265 years (1603–1868).

The underlying famous saying is "whoever wins be-comes the emperor's military, and those who lost were rebels". Japanese citizens automatically believed the vic-tor is on the side of the emperor and obeyed. *After World War II, MacArthur used this saying adroitly, probably without knowing it, and showed the Japanese that he is on the side of the emperor. It was the first time in her his-tory that a foreign warrior became the ruler of Japan, and he sided with the emperor by being photographed in public with the emperor. MacArthur defended the emper-or against other leaders of the allies who wanted to treat the emperor as a war criminal. The wisdom of the Ma-cArthur policy became quite apparent by the problems caused by the complete destruction of the Iraq govern-ment after the quick military victory by the Americans (2001).*

The lord of the Satsuma clan (present Kagoshima Pre-fecture at the southern end of Kyushu), Shimazu Naria-kira, felt that the way to avoid humiliation by European countries and America, as China had been subjected, was to learn their technologies as quick as possible and to become rich and militarily strong. He had motivated young samurais among his clan that the clan system led by Tokugawa Bakufu had to be replaced by a stronger centralized government. He felt that the only way to do this without a civil strife was to unite Japan under direct rule in the name of the emperor. His famous followers were Komatsu Tatewaki, Saigo Takamori, and Okubo

Toshimichi. Komatsu was an elder of the Satsuma clan, who acted as a liaison between lower ranked samurais Saigo and Okubo and Lord Shimazu, but he died soon after the Edo Castle was transferred to the emperor. Saigo Takamori was the most famous and respected of the three. He led the force that accepted the peaceful transfer of the Edo Castle, but disagreed with the policies of the new government. He was induced into fighting the government force led by his colleague and friend Okubo Toshimichi but lost and committed suicide in 1877. Okubo Toshimichi was a dominant figure involved in the formation of the Meiji government but was assassinated by the followers of Saigo the following year.

The most famous of the Choshu clan (present Yamaguchi Prefecture at southwestern end of Honshu) of this period was Kido Takayoshi. He was the leader of the Choshu clan that formed an alliance with the Satsuma clan to defeat Tokugawa force and directly involved in the formation of the new national government (Meiji Ishin, known in English as the Meiji restoration).

CHAPTER 31:
MEIJI ISHIN (RESTORATION)

31-1: Establishment of the Modern Japanese Government

Edo was renamed Tokyo, which means the East Capital. The Bakufu system, made up of 261 semiautonomous clans, was replaced by the prefectural system under the national government in 1871. The leaders of these clans became the nobility.

The reform of the national government (Meiji Ishin) was carried out under the leadership of samurais from the Satsuma and Choshu clans. Some samurais from the Tosa and Hizen clans (present Kochi Prefecture in Shikoku and Saga Prefecture in Kyushu, respectively) also made significant contributions.

The government sent the envoy led by Iwakura Tomomi with four associates, which included afore mentioned Okubo Toshiaki and Kido Takayoshi, to America,

England, and nine European countries; the trip took a year and a half (1871–1873). They were impressed by the American system of electing the leader by the votes of ordinary citizens but decided that the Japanese were not educated enough for it.

The envoy favored the constitutional monarchy of Germany under Kaiser rather than the democratic constitutional monarchy of England. Their proposal won over those that favored the British system. Therefore, Teikoku Gikai, their imperial legislature called "Imperial Diet" in English, followed the German legislature. It was a bicameral legislature—the House of Peers consisted of the nobilities, and the House of Representatives was elected by the eligible voters. The eligible voters were only males twenty-five years or older who paid taxes, only 1.14 percent of the population. They were mostly real estate owners. In 1925 the eligible voters were expanded to include all men older than twenty-five.

The executive branch was headed by the prime minister appointed by the emperor on the recommendation of the council of elders. The elders were the people involved in the Meiji Ishin and were mostly from the former Satsuma and Choshu clans. In the early period, the prime minister was selected from the members of elders. For the first seven prime ministers, leaders of the Choshu and Satsuma clans alternated taking the position of the prime ministers. However, the three leaders from the Satsuma clan that initiated the Meiji Restoration were dead by then, and Yamagata Aritomo and Ito Hirobumi of the Choshu clan were the most influential among the elders.

In 1885 Ito Hirobumi became the first prime minister; he was a member of Iwakura envoy (paragraph 3 and 4, this section). The prime minister formed his cabinet consisting of the ministers who were heads of various bureaus of the government, with the important exception that the ministers of the army and navy were named independent of the prime minister.

The Meiji Constitution, established in 1889, had placed the military and executive branches independent of each other directly under the emperor. The emperor followed the advice of elders, Therefore, the leaders from Satsuma and Choshu clans, who were involved in Meiji Restoration controlled both the government and military. The winners of the political parties served on the Imperial Diet, but did not have much influence as long as the elders were active.

The political parties were formed in 1881 to 1882, and the first election was held on July 1, 1890. The Constitutional Liberal party got the largest number of seats, and when combined with the Progressive Party, their combined total won 57 percent of the seats. They wanted to dislodge the Satsuma and Choshu clans from the leadership of the government, but Yamagata Aritomo was the prime minister at the time of the election and ignored the victors of the election in the formation of his cabinet.

In 1896 Itagaki Taisuke, the head of Constitutional Liberal Party, finally became a member of the cabinet, the Minister of the Interior, and later in the year, Okuma

Shigenobu from the Constitutional Progressive party became the Minister of Foreign Affairs. Both men were involved in the Meiji Restoration and, therefore, the elders, but were not from the Choshu or Satsuma clan. They were from Tosa and Hizen, respectively, and fought for the more democratic form of the government. Two years later they combined their parties and formed the cabinet with Okuma as the prime minister and Itagaki as the Minister of the Interior, the first cabinet formed by a political party. Other ministers were also from their parties and clans, except the ministers of the navy and army, which were from Satsuma and Choshu, respectively.

From then on political parties gradually dominated the positions for prime ministers and cabinet members. Therefore, the government gradually became independent of the elders. However, the ministers of the army and navy were still selected by the military leaders, who were still mostly from the Choshu and Satsuma clans. If the military advisers did not like the prime ministers, they refused to recommend the persons for the military ministers. This caused the failure of the formation of the cabinet. This process made it possible for the military to have a strong voice in government policy. The military became independent of the government, and as the elders from the Meiji Restoration faded away by aging and poor health, the communication between the government and military became almost nonexistent. The civilian government did not have any voice in military policies.

31-2: Formation of Imperial Military Force

At the beginning of the Meiji Restoration, the military was established under the conscription system for all men (1873) and the samurai class was abolished. The military was quickly modernized—the army learned from the Germans and the navy from the British. The military strategists learned from a German general that the way to win a war is to prepare for it and then to attack immediately after the declaration of the war (Tahara, 2000). The Japan-Qing War (1894–1895) and Russo-Japanese War (1904–1905) were won by this tactic. The first war prevented China from controlling Korea, and the second war stopped Russia from controlling Korea and Southern Manchuria. Therefore, these could be considered defensive wars. However, Japan got Taiwan from the first war and got South Sakhalin Island and transfer of the lease on Kwangtung (Liaodong) Peninsula south of Manchuria (Darien-Port Author) from Russia. They also got control of the railways in Manchuria from the Russians and established Mantetsu (South Manchurian Railway) where my father worked. By these two wars, Japan became recognized as a world military power and safe from the danger of invasion by a foreign power. The military got the respect of ordinary Japanese citizens; the citizens thought that the military conquest was a profitable venture.

If the military staff were wise and had better knowledge of international relationships, they would have stopped military aggression at this point. However, the military did not have wise, strong leaders. The Japanese were taught that they won the war because of the Yamato Spirit; they could defeat any force that had much superior quantitative and qualitative armament. In reality the Japanese won the Russo-Japanese War despite their inferior military force because of the diplomatic prearrangement for Theodore Roosevelt to intervene to cease the fighting prior to exhaustion of the military supply by the Japanese force.

31-3: Formation of National Education System

Prior to the Meiji Ishin, students were taught locally under a wise teacher. The emphasis was on gaining wisdom based on jukyo. *The elders from Meiji Restoration were wise but failed to educate their followers on wisdom and the importance of diplomacy.*

After the restoration, the central government established the education system unified under the Ministry of Education, and all the children were required to have six years of education. There were some private schools. They used the textbooks approved by the Ministry of Education. *This easily led to the control of the thoughts of the Japanese (brainwashing).*

The emperor proclaimed the purpose of education in 1890. This message stressed complete obedience to the emperor, who is the descendant of the Sun Goddess. In 1912 Nitobe Inazo had translated the message on education into English as "the basis for all moral teaching in school." Here is an excerpt from the translation: "Ye, Our subjects, be filial to your parents, affectionate to your brothers and sisters; as husbands and wives be harmonious, as friends true; bear yourselves in modesty and moderation; extend your benevolence to all; pursue learning and cultivate the arts, and thereby develop intellectual faculties and perfect moral powers." This message was read frequently before a student body. At the schools I attended in Manchuria, I listened to this message many times, but I do not remember on what occasions.

This was read to a student body with the photograph of the emperor in the front, and the students had to bow their heads throughout the reading. I was surprised to learn from Nitobe Inazo's book that the photograph was a photo of an oil painting of the emperor painted by an Italian artist. Uchimura Kanzo (chapter 23) was a high school teacher when the message was read the first time. He was a Christian and refused to bow his head because it would mean that the emperor is his god. He was fired from his position (*Japan Chronik*, 958). Later, I read about Chinese Christianity in *Taiping Heavenly Kingdom* (Reilly, 2010) that emperor means God. Therefore, he was justified in refusing to bow his head.

After the war the General Headquarters (GHQ) of the occupational force prohibited the reading of the message. This message was identified as a cause of the Japanese militarism. *However, the emperor's message is based on Confucian-Shinto teaching and ingrained in the Japanese mentality. Even today students tend to obey their teachers and tend to accept their teaching without asking questions. In my opinion the major defect was the nationally centralized education system, and the GHQ did not modify this system because it was the easy way to enforce its policy. This system is maintained even to this day.*

The GHQ should have prohibited the use of the word "Tenno" for the Japanese emperor. He is no longer considered God, but Tenno means emperor in heaven or God. This means the Japanese are still calling him God without being conscious of it. The Japanese have a different word for gods, kami, *which in Chinese means spirits, and the Japanese do consider gods as spirits. It is inappropriate to call the Christian God kami. However, Japanese Christians and their Bible call God kami, or spirit. According to the book by Reilly (2010), kami or spirits are considered lower than the emperor in heaven. Both the Japanese and Chinese do not distinguish singular and plural by the ending of a noun but it's understood by its context.*

CHAPTER 32:
BUDDING DEMOCRACY

The World War I economy brought high inflation. Housewives of a small farming village in Toyama Prefecture, on the central Japan Sea coast, demonstrated against the high price of rice. It soon spread throughout the nation and forced the Japanese cabinet to dissolve; it was the first time a democratic demonstration by ordinary citizens brought down the government.

The first commoner outside of the elders from the Meiji Reformation era, Hara Takashi, was appointed the new prime minister in 1918. He was the head of Seiyukai, a conservative party established in 1900 by Ito Hirobumi. It had the majority of the members of the House of Representatives, and the cabinet members were all from Seiyukai, except for the Ministers of Navy, Army, and Foreign Affairs. These ministers were appointed by separate recommendations to the emperor by the elders.

This period was known as Taisho Democracy, the era of the reign of the Taisho Emperor (1912–1926). The rice demonstration led to enhanced activities for social reforms, but Hara was too conservative to support these social reforms. His party won the large majority of the general election immediately following his premiership, but he actively tried to suppress the socialistic movement. He was assassinated by a railroad employee in 1921, the first assassination of the head of the government since Meiji Ishin.

From 1921 to 1932, nine prime ministers, six of whom were the leaders of three political parties, formed eleven cabinets. Each cabinet lasted on the average only one year. Japan was under a severe depression since the Great Kanto Earthquake in 1923. The nation was dragged into the worldwide depression started by the collapse of the New York Stock Exchange in 1929. Unfortunately, each party, or the combination of the parties, while in power was not able to do anything about it. The citizens perceived that these parties were increasingly corrupt and not interested in the well-being of the country but only in their own political parties. The Japanese were disillusioned by the rule of inept political parties.

The last of this series of prime ministers, Inugai Tsuyoshi, was assassinated by a group led by young navy and army officers in 1932 after serving only five months in office. He was the last political party leader to serve as the prime minister until after World War II. This made an opening for the military to take over the control of the government.

The economic recession and political instability in Japan ever since the economic bubble had busted in 1991 were similar. The government did not have stable leadership; there were six prime ministers in six years (September 2006–December 2012) accompanied by the Great Earthquake of East Japan (March 11, 2011). Since 2008, the whole economy of the developed world is under severe recession, and the Japanese economy was dragged into it. In my opinion the profit-driven capitalism that depends on consumer debts is not sustainable; it needs major reform.

CHAPTER 33:
MILITARISM

33-1: The Beginning of Militarism

The Manchurian Incident is considered the beginning of Japanese Military aggression; it was planned and executed by the staff of Kwantung army (Chapter 9). Neither the central government nor the central command in Japan was able to punish them. It would humiliate the Japanese military; pride was more important than the future consequence. *This in contrast to President Truman's firing of General MacArthur during the Korean War (1951) for his insisting to invade Manchuria. Truman was afraid that this might lead to a third world war. If the prime minister at the time of the Manchurian Incident had been strong enough to punish Itagaki and Ishihara, the instigators of the incident, Japan may have avoided the subsequent wars of aggression. It is important to note that the Japanese did not have strong leadership in the central government or in the military, and field military staff initiated the wars of aggression.*

The Japanese Army at Japanese-occupied outposts learned that military aggression could be initiated without getting permission from the central command. It is shocking that the field staff started Japanese aggressions without the knowledge of the central military staff, and they had no experiences in diplomacy. Inept political parties were to blame for losing the respect of the citizens. The military gained the respect of the Japanese citizens and media for their decisive actions.

The Manchu Incident led to the complete control of Manchuria by the Japanese; the Chinese consider this as the beginning of the fourteen-year war against Japan. The Japanese government went along with the Kwangtung Army and established Manchuko in 1932. The League of Nations refused to recognize Manchuko, and Matsuoka Yousuke, the representative to the League of Nations, withdrew Japan from the League in 1933. Japan was in the midst of the depression, and both the Japanese people and the press supported the action of the Kwantung Army to control resources of Manchuria and treated Matsuoka as a hero for the withdrawal from the League of Nations.

The Japanese enthroned the last Emperor of the Qing dynasty, Pu Yi, as the Emperor of Manchuko in 1934. Japanese civilians in Manchuko were taught that it would be a country for five ethnic groups to live in harmony as equals—Manchurian, Mongolian, Chinese, Korean, and Japanese. However, in reality the Japanese civilians did not think they were citizens of Manchuko but masters over other ethnic groups. Japanese students went to Japanese schools and were taught from the same textbooks as the students in Japan.

33-2: Actions that made the Pacific War Inevitable

The Japanese Army in North China, following the precedent of the Manchu Incident, caused the incident at Rokou Bridge (Marco Polo Bridge) near Beijing on July 7, 1937. They were carrying out a military practice at night. They heard a few real gunshots and decided that the Chinese military nearby shot at them and started to attack them. They used the incident as the excuse to invade further into the Chinese mainland. The Japanese side considered this as the beginning of the war against China. Even the instigator of the Manchu Incident, Ishihara Kanji, was against this war because he was concerned that the war would deplete the Japanese military's strength. His purpose for the control of Manchuria was to use it as the base to invade Siberia.

The initial purpose of the Japanese invasion into China was to establish North China into a country friendly to Japan. However, the initial phase of the military action was so successful that they refused to stop and kept on going deeper and deeper into China. The US government by this time was convinced that war against Japan was inevitable and encouraged Chiang Kai-Sheik to keep on fighting, hoping that would get the Japanese Army stuck in China, so they would not be capable of starting another war.

According to F. G. Wilson (1949), a professor of political science at the University of Washington while my father was studying there, the United States wanted China and Japan to be hostile to each other. If they formed an alliance, they would become too strong for the West to dominate the Pacific. Therefore, the United States encouraged the hostility between the two countries.

The purpose of the Kwangtung Army to establish Manchuko was to use is as the base to invade Siberia. However, they got involved in fighting the Russians at Nomonhan, Inner Mongolia, south of Hailar, and were defeated in 1939. They realized that the Russians had a highly mechanized army that they would not be able to match for at least five more years. Many military leaders were also aware that they could not win a war against America. However, the large majority of Japanese citizens and their leaders were brainwashed by their centralized education system into believing that with the Japanese spirit they could defeat enemies that had more superior armament.

The Germans invaded Poland, and the British and French declared war on Germany; World War II started in September of 1939. The Germans occupied Poland and France so quickly and drove out the British forces from the continent that the Japanese government decided that Germany would win the war.

Between 1935 and 1941, the critical period prior to World War II, the Japanese foreign policy was divided. Diplomats and the military agreed on one theme— they were against Communism. They were thinking of invading Siberia at an opportune time and wanted to gain control of natural resources in the Southeast Pacific, especially the oil in Indonesia. Britain, France, and the Netherlands were defeated or losing to the Nazis and would not be able to defend their colonies. They did not want to fight America to gain control of the Southeast Pacific.

They were undecided on the tactics to gain these objectives and to keep America neutral. The diplomats and some military factions wanted to stop the war against China. However, the military fighting in China did not want to withdraw, and instead kept on going deeper and deeper into China. The Japanese diplomats were powerless to do anything about it. The military got into diplomacy without notifying the foreign ministry. For example the Japanese military attaché at the Japanese Embassy in Berlin was smoothly forming an alliance with the Nazis against Soviet Russia but did not inform the foreign ministry.

Matsuoka Yosuke was appointed as the foreign minister at this crucial period (July 1940–July 1941) under the second Konoe cabinet. He was educated in America and fluent in English. He thought he could still mend the relationship with the United States and use her to stop war against Chang Kai-shek and China (Lu, 2002). Almost the first action he took was to form an alliance with Germany and Italy in September of 1940, and then he formed the nonaggression treaty with Russia in April of 1941. His actions placed Japan firmly on the opposite side of the British and Americans and made the war inevitable.

These actions puzzled me and induced me to read a book by David Lu (2002) on Matsuoka and the Japanese foreign policies of that period. In 1893, Matsuoka came to America, he was thirteen years old. He lived with a Methodist family in Portland, Oregon. His foster mother was a sister of the host. She treated him equally with her brother's children and taught him about the American way of life. He attended the University of Oregon from 1898 to 1900 and graduated with a law degree and went back to Japan in 1902.

He served as a secretary at the Japanese Embassy in Washington, DC from 1913 to 1916 and made trips across the American continent twice during that period. Then on the way back from the League of Nations in Geneva in 1933, he went across the United States giving speeches at several places in the front of large crowds. He received favorable coverage from the American press. These experiences as a student and diplomat gave him confidence that he knew Americans. He thought that the best way to deal with Americans was to express his opinion forcefully as an equal.

He became a foreign minister in the second Konoe cabinet in 1940. Konoe gave him a free hand in foreign policies. He thought he finally got a chance to improve the relationship with America and to stop the war against Chang Kai-shek and China. He formed an alliance with Germany and Italy to make Japan equal in power to the United States and England. He wanted to form the alliance with Russia, but the German invasion of Russia made that impossible. However, he succeeded in forming the nonaggression treaty with Russia. Konoe even agreed with him to disband all political parties and unite the government under one party to have unified policies. The removal of political parties made it easier for subsequent control of the government by the military.

Matsuoka was a loner and did all the policy making decisions by himself. The rest of the government leaders did not like this. American Ambassador Joseph Grew did not get along with him either. Anti-Matsuoka factions convinced Konoe that the pact with Russia would give the wrong impression that Japan is procommunist. Konoe dissolved his second cabinet to relieve Matsuoka of his position on July 18, 1941. Matsuoka was not able to meet with President Roosevelt. Both President Roosevelt and Matsuoka were waiting for the other side to initiate the meeting.

As subsequent history showed, all of Matsuoka's tactics backfired and made the war against the United States unavoidable. Apparently he was not aware that Chang Kai-shek did not want to stop the war against Japan and was getting aid from the United States because he was convinced that China could not fight Japan alone. His wife, Soon May-ling, was well-known for her effort to get aid from America. The US government gave them aid. However, the Americans also sold scrap irons and oil for the Japanese military industrial complex. Soon after the dismissal of Matsuoka, the Japanese military moved into Indochina on July 28, 1941. This caused America to finally stop the export of oil and scrap irons to Japan. This forced Japan to fight the United States to get to the oil in Indoneshia.

The Roosevelt administration thought as did the Japanese that the British would lose the war unless the Americans got into the war. However, America was not ready for war. To gain time the Roosevelt administration started negotiations with the Japanese to avoid the war. Both sides were half-hearted participants in the negotiation. Neither side liked the proposal made by the Secretary of State, Cordell Hull, but used it as the basis for the negotiations.

33-3: Great Far East War (the Japanese name for the Pacific War)

By this time the influence of the elders from Meiji Ishin was gone; the last remaining one, Saiongi kinmochi, who served as the prime minister (1906–1908, 1911–1912) and was known to fight against the military encroachment, was in ill health and died in November of 1940. When the elders were gone, the government did not have a voice in military policies and had very poor communication with the military. It was shocking that the Japanese government did not have a long-range policy and, after the military control, dealt with the international problems by military conquests. It should have been obvious to the leaders of the United States and Britain that the military controlled the Japanese government policies.

The Japanese military occupied Indochina in July of 1941. This angered the Americans and stopped oil and scrap iron export to Japan on August 1. *I learned recently from a program on NHK TV (circa 2012) that the Japanese were using gold to buy those items; perhaps that was the reason the Americans maintained trade with the militaristic Japan for so long.* The Japanese had only a year and a half of oil in reserve and eyed Indonesia as their source of oil. The Netherlands was occupied by the Nazis; she did not have the military strength to defend Indonesia.

Konoe Fumimaro, the last of the nonmilitary prime ministers, resigned on October 16 because he did not want to be the leader to start the war against the United States and Great Britain. The advisors to Emperor Hirohito recommended General Tojo Hideki as the prime minister, judging that he was the only one capable of influencing the military. Emperor Hirohito told Tojo, at the time of his appointment, to avoid war against America if possible. Tojo himself felt that the possibility of winning the war against America was small (Tahara, 2000).

The Americans demanded complete withdrawal of the Japanese from Indochina and China. Cordell Hull, the Secretary of State, handed the American ultimatum to the head of the Japanese delegation on November 26. The Japanese considered these conditions too humiliating to accept, and it should have been obvious to the US leaders that to the military-controlled Japanese government, the war was the only choice left.

On December 1 at a conference in the presence of Emperor Hirohito, the Japanese decided to start the war by attacking Pearl Harbor on December 8 (*Japan Chronik* 1991: 1076). The American government may have known of this action because it had broken the Japanese code. Hull pretended he did not know the content of the note when the Japanese delegates delivered the note soon after the Pearl Harbor attack. The Japanese government blamed the Japanese Embassy for the delay. The embassy did not use a typist and used it as the excuse in tardiness of the transmission.

American citizens were against the war, and many were sympathizers to the Nazis. Roosevelt was looking for a way to unite Americans to support the war. The Pearl Harbor attack made Americans unite and support the war with a vengeance. John Dower wrote that the attack was godsent (2010). He also wrote that the Democrats and Liberals were not aware that the Japanese were about to attack, but the Republicans and Conservatives thought that the Roosevelt administration had induced Japan to attack in order to get Americans to support the war.

Yamamoto Isoroku, the admiral of the combined fleet of the Japanese Navy, felt that if they destroyed the major fraction of the American naval force at Pearl Harbor, they could control the sea and air over the Pacific for about a year. The Japanese designed torpedoes that would work in shallow water like Pearl Harbor. Their major objective was to control the oil field of Indonesia.

The Pearl Harbor attack was coordinated with the invasion of the Philippines, Malay Peninsula, Indonesia, and Burma. The plan was perfectly executed (chapter 1). American citizens were surprised by the Pearl Harbor attack, but the surprise to the American leaders was the bold plan and simultaneous execution of the attacks on all these fronts. The United States Navy was surprised that Japan sank four battleships and damaged many others by specially designed torpedoes. The British Navy was surprised that their "unsinkable" battleship, Prince of Wales, was sunk on an open sea by planes. It is strange that even though the Japanese had shown for the first time that planes could sink battleships, they still built the world's largest battleships, Yamato and Musashi, white elephants.

The Japanese had attained their initial objective of the control of the South Pacific and the oil fields of Indonesia when the commander of the Netherlands Army surrendered unconditionally on March 9, 1942. The Japanese government was split between the further continuation of the attacks, favored by the navy, and the defense of the areas already occupied, favored by the army. The proposal by the navy won, and they decided to continue the attack, but they failed to make significant additional gains (Tahara, 2000).

At the battle off Midway Island on June 5, 1942, the Japanese fleet lost four aircraft carriers, while the Americans lost only one. The American force knew the position of the Japanese fleet due to the careless use of a telegraph by the Japanese and waited for the Japanese fleet. This battle was never reported to the Japanese public. I was not aware of the battle until I came back to the States.

The Japanese were drunk from the series of initial victories. Then, by the series of battles off the Solomon Islands, they lost their attacking capability, and they lost control of the air and sea by the beginning of 1943. Their defensive strategy did not work either. The Japanese were overextended, spread all over the southern Pacific islands, Southeast Asia, and the Aleutian Islands. Chang Kai-sheik had retreated to Chongqing and a major fraction of the Japanese Army was stuck in mud deep in Chinese mainland. The Japanese Navy and Air Forces were no longer able to match the American force by the number or quality. The Japanese forces scattered all over the Pacific were left to fend for themselves with whatever they had. Beginning with Attu Island in the Aleutian Islands on May 29, 1943, Japanese soldiers fought to the "last man" on every Japanese-held island in the Pacific that the American force landed. Saipan (July 7, 1944) and Iwo Jima (March 25, 1945) were the best known of these battles. Prior to the war, Tojo sent a message to the military that to be captured alive by the enemy is to bring shame to their country and families; it is better to die. Under this motto the Japanese fought to their deaths even when a battle was lost rather than surrender.

The combined fleet of the Japanese Navy made the last all-out attack against the American force off the Philippines as they were landing on Leyte Island, and they were almost completely destroyed, essentially the end of the Japanese Navy. At this battle off Leyte Island, kamikaze attacks were used for the first time on October 23, 1944. The kamikaze was the only means left for the Japanese to attack the American naval force. Kamikaze means divine wind, which was the name given to the typhoons that destroyed the Mongol invading forces twice in the thirteenth century.

Tragically, many promising college students and graduates died as kamikaze pilots. I met a former kamikaze pilot while waiting in line to tour Mont Saint-Michel in France in 2006, and the conversation with him induced me to read the diaries by Japanese kamikaze pilots (Emiko Ohnuki-Tierney, 2006). I was surprised to learn that even kamikaze pilots were against the war and were critical of the militarism and the imperial system. They were well-read on philosophy by Western and Japanese philosophers. One wrote that men of his generation were born to be killed and felt becoming a kamikaze was the best way to kill more of the enemy as he died. One predicted already in 1942, at the height of the Japanese victories, that Japan would be defeated. One wrote that Japan, corrupted by zaibatsu (rich families that controlled the Japanese economy), had to be destroyed completely so that a new Japan would rise from the ashes.

Tojo failed to follow what he preached. After the war, at the time of his arrest, he tried to commit suicide by shooting himself but failed. For a samurai to fail to commit suicide was a disgrace. Tojo brought shame to himself. *One day while living in Oak Ridge, Shigeko and I visited a carpet store in Dalton, Georgia. A sales person of the store told us that he was guarding Tojo when he tried to commit suicide.*

Even in Manchuria after the Russian invasion, the Japanese soldiers defended the forts along the Siberian boarder until they were killed or until the war ended. The defenders of the forts along the northeast border of Manchuria were not aware that the Russian invasion was real until the Russians passed by them (Handou, 2002).

The main forces were ordered to retreat to the Korean border to defend Korea and to defend Japan's main islands against the Russians. They ignored the Japanese civilians in Manchuria. They caused tragedy among the Japanese farmers recruited to cultivate the farmlands. The military took away the farms from the Manchurians and gave the farms to the Japanese to cultivate. Then they drafted many young farmers into the army. As soon as the war was over, the Manchurians took back the farms. The farmers and their children escaped by foot. Many of these were killed or died of cold and starvation. Some Manchurians adopted children who were left behind.

I was not aware until recently that the primary duty of the Japanese military was to defend the emperor, not the civilians. Civilians could be sacrificed to save the emperor. The emperor owned Japan. The citizens were his subjects, and their duty was to serve the emperor, even by sacrificing their lives. *The young generations of the present era do not understand this mentality. The postwar Japanese citizens learned that under democracy, the citizens own their country; they are the boss.*

Even a young Japanese history researcher thought the Japanese Army's duty was to protect Japan's citizens. I met this person in Hailar while we were on the tour (chapter 9). I told him that the invasion of China was aggression. He got mad at me and said that the war was to protect the Japanese citizens being harassed by the Chinese. Based on my observations in Manchuria, that could not have been the real motive.

33-4: Japanese Americans in the Pacific War

By executive order in the spring of 1942, the Americans of Japanese ancestry, even those with American citizenship, were forcibly removed from the West Coast to camps in desolate inlands. About 110,000 of them were moved to ten camps with minimal amounts of personal belongings. They lost their farms, businesses, and jobs. My grandparents were sent to the camp in Minidoka, Idaho. They lost Hotel Diller located at the corner of the First Avenue and University Street, near Pike market. The business was thriving with no vacancies every night. Yet, they never complained to us about their experiences.

Recently (circa 2012), I saw a documentary about the Japanese American experiences on TV, and those interviewed of my generation, Nisei*, said that their parents did not tell them much about their experiences. Nisei means second generation; I am Sansei from the Fujimuras, or my mother's side. My generation is mostly Nisei and Sansei Americans. Many of these that went to the camps were sensitized to discrimination by racial profiling. Perhaps the most prominent saying by these* *is Norman Mineta. He served as the Secretary of Commerce at the time of 9/11. He criticized the discrimination of Middle East Americans by racial profiling at the airports. He was on* 60 Minutes *and told the listeners not to use racial profiling to discriminate. Many Americans did. My car mechanic while I was in Miami was a Pakistani; he complained to me that soon after 9/11 he was kicked in a store by a customer who thought he was an Afghan.*

The best-known heroics by the Japanese Americans during World War II were by the 442nd Regimental Combat Team and the 100th Infantry Battalion at the European front. The members of the units were the most decorated of the American troops. President Truman told the Nisei during a ceremony in their honor, "You fought not only the enemy, but you fought prejudice—and you won" (Hosokawa, 1969).

However, Nisei contributions during the war may have been more significant on the Pacific front, but the public did not know much about it. They were the Japanese Americans who served in military intelligent service (MIS). The veterans of MIS were prohibited from talking about their exploit for fifty years. One of them was in Oak Ridge; he grew up in Hawaii and told me that he was an MIS but did not tell me what he did. He said the most famous MIS was Donald Keene, who became a professor at Columbia University and was a well-known authority on Japanese art and literature. *He became a Japanese citizen in 2012. I was surprised to hear an NHK TV program on Hawaiian Nisei who fought as MIS in the battle of Imphal, India (September 12, 2012). I thought only the British fought battles on the Indian front; apparently Americans did too.*

We happened to live in Rockville, Maryland, about fifty years after the war (chapter 18). We went to Faith UMC in Rockville where we befriended Hank and Seiko Wakabayashi. Hank served in the MIS, and I learned about the MIS from him and a book he gave to me: *MIS in the War Against Japan* (Falk and Tsuneishi, 1995). On the islands the Americans invaded, the Japanese soldiers did not expect that the Americans would understand Japanese. They did not destroy or hide the documents about their strategies and openly discussed their plans. Their codes were also broken. The MIS could sneak onto their side and overhear or read their plans. Japanese prisoners easily divulged the information they had. Apparently, they were surprised that there were Japanese Americans who could read and speak Japanese and knew Japanese culture; these were called *Kibei*. They were educated in the Japanese schools and came back to America. Accordingly, the Americans knew about the enemy strategies and locations much better than in the European fronts.

The MIS had contributed significantly to the American victories. According to President Truman, they shortened the war by two years. One interviewed on the TV program cited above said that he preferred to fight on the Pacific front to show that he is a loyal American and willing to kill a Japanese, yet they showed compassion to the surrendered Japanese in their language and were appreciated by them. A sufficient number of the

Japanese surrendered. In the NHK program cited above, one Nisei veteran said that many Japanese civilians and soldiers came out of caves in Okinawa and surrendered when they heard instructions to surrender in Japanese. The Americans ceased fire to save those that came out; a few civilians who came out of the cave asked to extend the cease-fire period because there were more in the cave. They granted the extension as long as possible, but some did not come out and were killed.

The book contained many stories of the experiences of the MIS veterans, and I learned that they served as valuable bridges between the Americans and the captured Japanese. They also served as interpreters and translators of Japanese documents after the war in Japan. Many of them were Kibei, who had facilitated the understanding of the Japanese culture and behaviors by the occupational force. One story I read that surprised me was that one found canned tuna and rice among the captured Japanese military belongings on an island and had a feast of a Japanese dish. Until then the only stories I heard were that the Japanese were starved, eating snakes and whatever they could find.

My father also served with the title "supreme translator" at the GHQ in Tokyo for about one and a half years after his family had gone to America (1948–1949); he worked until his position was closed, presumably, when his job was finished. I wish he had told me about his experience.

As I finished writing this section, I learned that nineteen thousand of the Japanese Americans who served on three military units—100th Infantry Battalion, 442nd Regiment, and MIS—received the Congressional Gold Medal on November 10, 2011. The honor was long overdue but appreciated by those who were still living.

33-5: The End of the War

By 1944 the Japanese had feelers out for peace via the Russian government, but they should have known that the Americans were not willing to quit until they had avenged the Pearl Harbor attack to their satisfaction. The Japanese probably did not have any choice but to keep on fighting until the American side was satisfied that the Japanese were completely defeated, unconditionally. The most important reason for the Japanese not to accept the unconditional surrender was to preserve the imperial system. For the allied forces, only an unconditional surrender was acceptable.

Helen Mears wrote in her book *Mirror for Americans: Japan* (1948) that the battles over the Pacific islands were not essential for the American victory, and the American soldiers lost their lives fighting unnecessary battles over little islands. The Japanese would have withered themselves, if left alone, unable to ship essential food and resources to the home islands. They were not self-sufficient, and many would have died of starvation. This may have been a wise tactic, but it would have been unthinkable to the Americans even though it would have saved the lives of many soldiers. It required the development and the use of atomic bombs to induce the Japanese to surrender. Clinton Laboratories, the predecessor of

Oak Ridge National Laboratory, were created to develop atomic bombs. Soon after the attack on Pearl Harbor, the Army Corp of Engineers selected the land between Black Oak Ridge to the north and the Clinch River to the south in the mountains of East Tennessee as one of the three sites to develop the atomic bomb. The residents in four villages in the area were removed by court order in early 1942 (Johnson and Schaffer, 1994). Atomic bombs were used to kill defenseless, unsuspecting civilians including children. However, the bombs quickly ended the war, saving more than a million lives, including the Fujimuras, from the invading Russian armies in Manchuria.

At noon on August 15, 1945 (Japan time), the Japanese heard the voice of Emperor Hirohito over radios saying the war had ended. Women that had gathered around our radio wept. The transformation of the Japanese citizens, from believing that they could never be defeated to becoming quiet sheep under occupational forces, was dramatic. Soldiers everywhere quit fighting when they heard the broadcast. Just a single broadcast by the emperor to end the war did it. More than a million Japanese civilians came back safely from Manchuria, and more than a couple of million came back from other parts of Asia. These evacuees came back to the overcrowded country where more than sixty cities were flattened by air raids. People were starving, even with some aid from America. The end to militarism was dramatic and complete.

However, many did not hear and kept on fighting or hiding. On Guam a soldier came out of a cave about twenty years later. While I was visiting Hailar on

June 25, 2007 (chapter 9), one of the members of the tour was a defender of the fort surrounding Hailar. He told us that he fought at least for a week after the end of the war and surrendered; he was taken to Siberia then came back alive to Japan.

I read recently that the Japanese soldiers were not disarmed immediately after surrendering, but many were used to maintain peace and order in the areas they had occupied or participated as combatants on both sides in the civil wars that had erupted (Dower, 2010). In the War of Independence by the Indonesians from the Dutch, and in the initial phase of the Vietnam War between Ho Chi Minh and the French, the Japanese soldiers were on both sides.

I was shocked by the arrogance of former colonial powers to attempt to reestablish their colonies. Natives of the former colonies found out how easy it was for the Japanese to get rid of these former colonial powers, and they successfully fought for their independence. Therefore, the Japanese lost the war but succeeded in their objective to get rid of the former colonial powers from Southeast Asia.

In China a part of the Japanese soldiers that had surrendered to the Communist Chinese was incorporated into their army, as I had observed (chapter 4). A part of those that had surrendered to the Nationalists was incorporated into their army. Mao Zedong was the supporter of peasants' rights prior to becoming a Communist. He became the leader of the Communist party during the guerrilla war against the Japanese. Mao succeeded in gaining control of China and made it truly independent and free of foreign influence in 1949. We in America thought that the Russians helped them. However, the Soviet Russia was uneasy of the Chinese Communists and did not help in their fight against the Nationalists. The Russians gave up Manchuria to the Nationalists, as I had observed in Qiqihar in 1946. The Russians became the true ally of the Chinese Communists only after they won and aided their military to modernize to fight against America.

CHAPTER 34:
POSTWAR JAPAN UNDER THE AMERICAN UMBRELLA

After coming back from Manchuria to Japan occupied by allied forces, I observed Hiroshima and Tokyo ruined by the bombings. I came back to the United States on January 17, 1948. Since then, throughout my adult life, I have visited Japan occasionally, staying from about a week to fourteen months. I observed firsthand the rise of Japan from ashes to become an economic superpower.

Most of the people were satisfied and happy to live on the beautiful islands enjoying four seasons under the umbrella of the powerful United States of America.

The earthquake and tsunami of March 11, 2011, awoke the Japanese to the vulnerability of their country. They realized that each of them was too self-centered. They need to cooperate and form a bond as a nation to maintain their standard of living. The awakening of a sleeping tiger, China, and the doubt of the United States to defend Japan unless the American security is clearly threatened, is making the Japanese realize that the American umbrella is fading away.

My first memory of Japan was as an evacuee from Manchuria, October 11, 1946. Hofu was not bombed, but the white wall around my uncle's house had stripes of red paint as camouflage from B29 bombers. Tokyo was flat, but the area around Uncle Yoshiwada's house on a hill in Shibuya was one of the areas saved. People were half-starved. We left for America on January 7, 1948.

I observed directly Japan's rise from the ashes by visiting Japan as a scientist at key stages of recovery. The first visit was about fourteen years later when I went to Japan as a postdoctoral fellow at Osaka University (chapter 13). Thanks to the Korean War, the Japanese economy had revived and was booming. New constructions were going on at several places, and the air was full of dust. I followed the custom of the Japanese and wore a white shirt, tie, and suits to work. The neckline of the shirt was darkened from dust by the time I got home. People were busy commuting to work, dispersing from the Osaka railroad station. My colleagues at the laboratory were hard workers, but their salaries were very low; with the exchange rate of 360 yen to a dollar, the monthly stipend from my fellowship was higher than that of my professor. However, they were ambitious and dreaming of going to America to do research and to compete with the best.

The next visit to Japan was in 1967. I received a travel grant to attend the International Congress of Biochemistry in Tokyo. I went along with several members of the Biology Division of ORNL. By then Japan had highly efficient bullet train system connecting major industrial and business centers of Japan. However, the exchange rate was still 360 yen to a dollar. We enjoyed our visits. For many of my colleagues, it was the first and the only visit to Japan.

In 1981 I went to Japan as a fellow of Japan Society for the Promotion of Science (chapter 16-3). The plane fare was for the first class, which was sufficient to convert it into the economy class for Shigeko and me. By then the value of the yen was rising; it was 215 yen to a dollar. However, I was paid in yen, so it did not matter. I traveled mainly by the bullet trains southwest from Tokyo to give nine lectures at major universities and research institutes along the way; I even found time to visit Kawamuras and my former teacher and classmates in Hofu. I observed that Japan had fully recovered and had become a top scientific research center of the world.

From 1985 to 1986, the US government was concerned that the level of Japanese science and technology was gaining ground on America. I was asked to go to Japan to assess Japanese biotechnology with a diplomatic title. I gladly accepted because I am indebted to America for the wonderful life I was having. My father, who had the degree in political science from the University of Washington, would have been surprised if he was living. He had a proper degree but never served in any government offices neither in the United States nor Japan. I was posted at the American Embassy in Tokyo and visited major companies, universities, and research institutes. I observed firsthand levels of Japanese science and technology and the vitality of the economy. However, I concluded and reported that Japan may be number two, but still way behind the United States.

Japan did rise from the ashes, and the survivors of the war gained freedom by the complete defeat of the military and destruction of military industries. They got democracy and undreamed-of wealth; their standard of living rose quickly to equal that of the American and West European middle class. Japanese goods have spread all over the world and gained a reputation for their excellent quality. Their sciences and technologies attained the top levels in the world. I doubt they could have attained this level of success without getting rid of their military, military-industrial conglomerates, and absent landowners. Dr. Sohei Kondo, while in Oak Ridge, told me that the advantage the Japan got by the defeat was that the best brains in the country could concentrate on the development of the country and new consumer goods, while the Americans have to spend their best brainpowers and resources for military research and development.

In retrospect I was posted at the American Embassy in Tokyo when the Japanese economy was at its peak, and everyone I met was ambitious striving to attain the top in his or her field. Soon after that the economic bubble had busted; the stock prices went down to about one-quarter of the maximum. However, ordinary people were not affected by the fall in stock values. They kept on enjoying life with no apparent effect from the low growth rate of their economy. We have arrived at the age of instant communication. I could interact with my friends and relatives anywhere by e-mail. Shigeko prefers Japanese TV programs; so we subscribe to NHK TV and saw instantly the conditions of the Japanese economy and politics and learned their culture. We kept up with our relatives and friends in Japan as if we lived there. We became more aware of this at the time of the earthquake and tsunami disaster of March 11, 2011. We watched, transfixed on our TV, the live coverage of the disaster. I was amazed that the American TV reporters showed more emotion than the NHK reporters.

I interacted with the survivors of the East Japan disaster of 3.11 and the volunteers that assisted them (chapter 29-2). In the past visits to Japan, I interacted with scientists and relatives. On this occasion, I interacted with ordinary people and young students and learned their concerns and interests. The young volunteers sensed that 3.11 was their life course changing event. They learned from the experience that they need to bound together and cooperate. I felt that these young volunteers would be responsible leaders of the future.-However, there are defects in their systems, and I am perturbed that the American systems are following their path. I do not like their education system, which was unified under the Ministry of Education during the Meiji Restoration. Grade school students were taught to trust and obey superiors and experts. This has not changed, even under the postwar democracy. At sharing periods of the volunteers at the Ishinomaki Support Center, the participants were told not to ask questions. I thought that was the best time to discuss our experiences, but we were told just to listen. I was told that questions would inhibit presenters to tell freely what they really felt.

Japanese school systems evaluated the students based on national examinations. This is an excellent system for producing studious followers but not independent thinkers and leaders. I think this is the reason Japan did not have any wise political leaders to lead the country with foresight ever since the elders of the Meiji Restoration were gone. This led to the war that their leaders thought they could not win. Their military had an excellent initial battle plan but no long-range plans. *President Bush got into the Iraq War the same way; the only difference was that the Americans fought a small country already incapacitated by the first war; Iraq had no capacity to attack. I am dismayed that the American education system is becoming unified under the standardized examinations. The students are learning how to study just to improve grades. This will destroy their originality and independent thinking.*

The Japanese military with the support of their willing citizens led Japan into ruin that sacrificed more than three million people. After the defeat of Japan, Yoshida Shigeru was credited as the wise and strong-willed leader to lead the Japanese out of the ruin and chaos. I do not think so; I think the survivors of the war led themselves to undreamed-of prosperity despite the absence of leaders. I heard that those that evacuated from Manchuria contributed significantly in the recovery of Japan using their experiences in modernizing Manchuria.

The war ended in the best way possible for the Fujimuras in Manchuria. Thanks to our grandparents, we came back safely to America, and as described in this story, our lives were wonderful, far better than we could dream. Our grandparents persevered through discrimination and the injustice of being taken to Minidoka, a concentration camp. They quietly endured hardship so that their descendants would have good lives. Most of the Issei worked hard so that their descendants would have a college education and better life. Our parents' stable life ended with the war, and they never recovered to have the family independent of our grandparents. My siblings and I grew up without our father because of the American policy. We are indebted to our grandparents and mother for providing security during the turbulent but important period of our growth. I led my adult life as a curiosity-driven researcher without worrying about my wage and research funding; they were adequate. I think this was possible only in America of the period in which I lived.

It is ironic that I spent most of my professional life at Oak Ridge National Laboratory, the birthplace of atomic bombs, and our children grew up in Oak Ridge. We are thankful that the Russian Communists gave up attempts to dominate the world without fighting. It saved us from the nuclear destruction of our civilization. I wish that the Japanese government prior to the Pacific War were wise enough to comply with the American demands instead of fighting. A shrewd leader like Tokugawa Ieyashu would not have gone into a war that he knew he had very little chance of winning.

The ordinary Japanese live so well in peace and freedom that they are not aware that their country is under the protection of the American military. A famous episode that I read recently was that the governor of Tokyo, Ishihara Shintaro, who is one year older than I, was shocked to overhear on a commuter train a conversation between two students. One asked the other whether there was ever a war between Japan and America. If there was a war, who won? The governor was so shocked that he got off the train. The students may have been talking in jest. However, it is true that the common Japanese who survived the war were winners; they got undreamt-of freedom and prosperity that they could not have gotten under the military regime. Many of the Japanese born under the reign of the present emperor (Heisei era, 1988–present) are not aware that more than three million of their grandparents and great grandparents sacrificed their lives believing that unless they armed and defended their country, she would have been colonized.

After almost seventy years, their country is still defended by the Americans, who are considered as allies but who had continuously maintained bases in their country. The presence of American military force is almost invisible, except for the people of Okinawa. However, there are still many signs that Japan lost the terrible war initiated by them. The foremost sign is the skeleton of the dome of the former trade center near the epicenter of the atomic bomb dropped over Hiroshima. Okinawa has large American military bases, about 20 percent of the landmass of Okinawa. The Japanese have not signed a peace treaty with the Russians because they have not returned four islands at the southern end of the Kurile Islands. Former residents of those islands are dying, and I think the Japanese missed the chance when they did not get the islands back at the time of the collapse of Soviet Union. If the Japanese really want these islands, they should buy them.

The policy of the Iraq War revealed that the policy of the GHQ of the MacArthur-led Allied occupational forces was wise in keeping the Japanese bureaucracy intact and let them micromanage Japan. The bureaucrats gained freedom and power to govern after the military and economic conglomerates were gone. Major political parties after the war were a reformation of the parties disbanded by the Japanese government in 1940. Their faults, prior to the war and to the present, were that they were interested too much in their own party politics.

I credit nuclear bombs for ending the Cold War without another world war. Now that the Russian threat is gone, we should reduce the budget used for the military industrial complex. It is too excessive; the US military budget is larger than the rest of the world combined. Our nuclear arsenal is excessive; we could not justify the use of even one bomb. We should remove nuclear bombs and then tell the rest of the world that possesses them to get rid of them. I may be too idealistic to think they would obey.

The rise of China and India reveals that the Japanese can no longer live under the umbrella of America. I hope that Japan will produce independent and farsighted leadership to deal in cooperation and peaceful competition with America, Korea, China, India, and the rest of the world. Could America deal with the new powers as friends not enemies? Would Caucasian Americans trust Asians enough to share the Pacific as equals in peace and harmony? Would American military forces ever withdraw from Japan? Would future Americans be able to sustain the level of the middle-class standard that our generation enjoys? We need to develop science and technology to spread our level of the living standard to the rest of the world and to sustain it. We need to develop our own scientists and engineers without depending on that of foreign countries.

Helen Mears wrote (1948) that the Japanese were good students, learned to cope with foreign threats by military might, and got resources by colonizing neighbors. They were punished for being good students. The Japanese were the mirrors of the Euro-American powers. I would say that the Japanese are still their mirror; Japan is not considered as one of the Asian countries. The Japanese have encountered ahead of others the economic bubble, the need for alternate sources of energy, the aging of the population, etc. The rest of the world could learn from them, usually their mistakes, in how not to deal with these problems and to develop sustainable Planet Earth economically and ecologically in peace and harmony.

REFERENCES

Andraos N., S. Tabor, and C. C. Richardson. "The Highly Processive DNA Polymerase of Bacteriophage T5." *Journal of Biological Chemistry* 279 (2004): 50609–50618.

Behe, Michael. *Darwin's Black Box*. Simon & Schuster, 1998

Borg, Marcus J. *The God We Never Knew: Beyond Dogmatic Religion to a More Authentic Contemporary Faith*, Harper One, 1998 (196 pages)

Burgers PM and 20 others. "Eukaryotic DNA polymerases. Proposal for a revised nomenclature" Journal of Biological Chemistry 276 (2001): 43487-43490.

Caldarola, Carlo. *Christianity: The Japanese Way*, 1979

Das S. K. and R. K. Fujimura. "Processiveness of DNA polymerases: A comparative study using a simple procedure." *Journal of Biological Chemistry* 254 (1979): 1227–1232.

Dower, John W. *Cultures of War*, W. W. Norton & Company 2010

Falk, Stanley L. and Tsuneishi, Warren, eds. *MIS in the War Against Japan*. Japanese American Veterans Association of Washington, DC, 1995.

Fujimura, R. and P. Kaesberg. "The Adsorption of Bacteriophage φX174 to Its Host." *Biophysical Journal* 2 (1962): 433–449.

Fujimura, R. K., S. Das, D. P. Allison, B. C. Roop. "Replication of Linear Duplex DNA in Vitro with Bacteriophage T5 DNA Polymerase" in *Progress in Nucleic Acid Research and Molecular Biology*, Edited by Waldo E Cohn 26 (1981): 49–62.

Fujimura, Robert. *Biotechnology in Japan*; International Trade Administration, Washington, DC, National Technical Information Service, US Department of Commerce (1988): PB89-141147 (178 pages).

Fujimura, Robert K. *Research and Development in Biotechnology-Related Industries in Japan.* Prepared by the US Department of Commerce Technology Administration Japanese Technical Literature Program. National Technical Information Service, US Department of Commerce (1989): PB89-167936 (55 pages).

Fujimura, Robert K "Chapter V: Viral Load on HIV-1 Associated Dementia: Neuropathology and Drug Efficacy". *In Neuro-AIDS.* Edited by A. Minagar and P. Shapshak, (2006) 101-119.

Fujimura, Robert. K., Teresita Reiner, Gangchao Ma, Virginia Phillips, Alicia de las Pozas, Dennis W. Dickson, Bernard A. Roos, Guy A. Howard, and

Carlos Perez-Stable. "Changes in the Expression of Genes Associated with Intraneuronal Amyloid-β and Tau in Alzheimer's Disease." *J Alzheimer's Disease* 19 (2010): 97–109.

Greene, Brian. *The Fabric of the Cosmos: Space, Time, and the Texture of Reality.* Vintage Book, 2004.

Handou, Kazutoshi. *The Summer Soviet Russia invaded Manchuria* (Japanese) Bunshuu Press. 2002.

Hosokawa, Bill. *Nisei: The Quiet Americans.* New York: William Morrow and Company, 1969 (522 pages).

Johnson, Leland. and Daniel. Schaffer. *Oak Ridge National Laboratory, The First Fifty Years.* Knoxville: University of Tennessee Press, 1994 (270 pages).

Kornberg, Arthur. *For the Love of Enzymes*, 1989.

Lehman, Robert. "T5 DNA Polymerase" in *The Enzymes* XIV, Part A, (1981) 60–62,

Lu, David J. *Agony of Choice, Matsuoka Yosuke and the Rise and Fall of the Japanese Empire, 1880–1946.* 2002.

Mears, Helen. *Mirror for Americans, Japan.* 1948.

Mitobe, Inazo. *The Japanese Nation, Its Land, Its People, and Its Life.* 1912.

Ohnuki-Tierney, Emiko. *Kamikaze Diaries—Reflections of Japanese Student Soldiers.* University of Chicago Press.2006 (254 pages).

Reilly, Thomas H. *Taiping Heavenly Kingdom.* The University of Washington Press 2010.

Shapshak, Paul, David M. Segal, Keith A. Crandall, Robert K. Fujimura, Bao-Tong Zhang,Ke-Qin Xin, Kenji Oluda, Carol K. Petito, Carl Eisdorfer, and Karl

Goodkin. "Independent Evolution of HIV Type 1 in Different Brain Regions." *AIDS Research and Human Retroviruses* 15 (1999): 811–820.

Spong, John S. *Why Christianity Must Change or Die.* Harper Collins, 1999

Sundberg, Albert C. Jr. "The Making of the New Testament Canon", *The Interpreter's One-Volume Commentary on the Bible.* Edited by C. M. Laymon. Abington Press, 1971: 1216–1224,

Tahara, Souichiro. *Japan's Wars* (Japanese). 2000.

Takayanagi, M. and M. Watanabe. *Japanese History by the Christian Centuries*, (Japanese). Meiji Shoin Ltd, 1958 (468 pages).

Takeuchi, Thomas, ed. *Minidoka Interlude*, Published by Residents of Minidoka Relocation Center, Hunt Idaho,1989.

The Illustrated Encyclopedia of American Cooking by The Editors of Favorite Recipes Press, Southwestern/Educational Marketing Services, Inc., 1983 (960 pages).

Uno, Shunichi, and seven other editorial members. *Japan Chronik: Complete History of Japan*, Kodansha LTD (Japanese). 1991 (1275 pages).

Volkin, E. and L. Astrachan, "Intracellular distribution of Labeled RNA after phage infection of E. coli." *Virology* 2 (1956): 433–437.

Volkin, Elliot. and L. Astrachan. "RNA Metabolism in T2-Infected ESCHERICHIA COLI" in *The Chemical Basis of Heredity.* Edited by McElroy & Glass (1957): 686–695.

Wilson, Francis G. *The American Political Mind: a Text-book in Political Theory*, 1949.